Entrepreneurial Investing

ENTREPRENEURIAL INVESTING

CONNECTING SOPHISTICATED CAPITAL WITH TALENTED SMALL BUSINESS

Callum Laing

RƎTHINK PRESS

First published in Great Britain in 2020
by Rethink Press (www.rethinkpress.com)

Illustrations originated by Charlotte Williams

Cover image © Copyright Shutterstock | Champ008

Praise

'Investors complain of not enough deal flow, business owners that there is never enough capital to expand. This book provides an excellent example of an innovative solution that marries the two. If you're serious about your investing, then you need to understand how this model works and how it can work for you.'

— **Dean Lindal,** Co-Founder and Director, DealGateway

'Many talk about the problem of over-dependence of SMEs on bank financing. Many also note that the "holy grail" for SMEs would be to be able to access capital markets, like larger firms. However, despite efforts over many years, including forming specialised stock exchanges in many countries (and the EU), little has changed. Callum Laing puts forward a new approach that may represent a breakthrough, a way to connect experienced entrepreneurs and the capital they can mobilise to SMEs. Is this the game changer in SME financing? Read his book to learn more.'

— **Matthew Gamser,** CEO, SME Finance Forum

'From interning in the back office of Barclays Bank in Cambridge, England, to working for an internet company at the height of the dot-com boom, Callum walks us through his entrepreneurial journey of finding a more sustainable business model. For him, that opportunity would be found in a segment that creates half the world's GDP – small businesses. In his quest to tap this obvious potential, Callum discovers the "holy trinity" of investing – connecting smart money to huge value-creation opportunities. In his latest book, Callum shares his insights on how each one of us can be part of creating sustainable businesses, have an impact and generate huge returns for ourselves and for society at large. A must-read for both investors and entrepreneurs.'

— **Kaiser Naseem,** International Development Banker

'Callum breaks through the "established norms" of typical investor thinking. He provides concepts and insights related to investing in an underutilised investment market with unlimited potential and opportunities. I particularly like the three circles analogy and avoiding the extremes and seeking the middle for value.'

— **Mike Newton,** Co-founder, JVFocus.com

'A growing number of high-net-worth individuals say values, not only profits and liquidity, drive their investment-making decisions. In his book *Entrepreneurial Investing*, Callum Laing shows a clear path to satisfying all three. He explains the economics of agglomeration in easy to understand terms, while telling a personal story that is both enlightening and entertaining.'

   — **Lana Coronado,** investor,
     CoronadoResults.com

'Callum is the master of simplifying complicated concepts. If you are an entrepreneur or investor, this book will open your eyes to a trillion-dollar opportunity that no one is talking about! It is a *must read*!'

   — **Victor Binitie,** The CEO Capital

'*Entrepreneurial Investing* is an exciting new book from author and entrepreneur Callum Laing. It is refreshing to see a book about entrepreneurial companies that is targeted at sophisticated investors. With his three circles model of Liquidity, Impact and Alpha, Callum identifies the sweet spot at the intersection of the three where there is a real opportunity for investors to achieve great returns and minimise risk.'

   — **David B Horne,** entrepreneur and Amazon
     bestselling author of *Add then Multiply*

'I can only say brilliant approach! *Entrepreneurial Investing* smartly addresses the current, unique market opportunity by enabling global capital to be deployed into small businesses, which are the lifeblood of the economy. An asset class is created which enables entrepreneurs to invest, make an impact and profit from it. In addition, I acknowledge Callum and his team in their persistence in working through the breakdowns and for making an impact in current and coming years.'

— **Goran Pregelj,** investor and global entrepreneur

'As an investor it's incredibly exciting, there are many, many great small businesses out there that are well run, profitable, and with significant potential. This model opens the gates to help them and to profit from them! Callum has a great talent for taking what should be a complex subject, simplifying it and demonstrating an otherwise previously overlooked opportunity!'

— **Karl Paul,** Managing Director of Smarter Media Ltd, www.smarter-media.co.uk

Contents

Introduction

This book is intended for you the *investor*. Or more specifically, those investors who want to profit from the explosion of what some have called the 'entrepreneurial revolution' – the combination of talent and opportunity and the tools to capitalise on them that is propelling the small business ecosystem. But unlike the myriad of books written for the budding entrepreneur, this book is designed for those who want to profit from the opportunity through investing capital, not investing blood, sweat and tears at the coalface.

To an entrepreneur/small business owner, the world of finance and investing can appear weird. You may have spent your whole career in the industry and to you it seems perfectly normal, but to us outsiders there is some strange stuff going on. And it's not entirely surprising that it's not the most beloved of industries in the world. But that's alright, this book hasn't been written to criticise the industry, but rather to point out what looks like a kink in the system which will for a period of time offer quite unparalleled returns. Like all great profit opportunities, I have no doubt that once the market realises the opportunity, the competition will rush in and the profits will be no more, but the size of this opportunity appears so large I think you, the savvy investor, have many years to enjoy it. However, I'm getting ahead of myself.

I'm not 'of' the industry. I didn't study finance or economics, I haven't got an MBA in advanced financial models, and I didn't cut my teeth as an intern for one of the prestigious investment banks for eighty hours a week.

And yet, somehow, I have found myself thrust into this weird world you call home. I create publicly listed companies. In the last few years I have generated hundreds of millions of dollars of value through mergers and acquisitions (M&A) and I have set up a fund based on an idea so seemingly simple and profitable that most people in the industry barely believed it would work.

The problem with being an outsider writing about the industry is that you will laugh at my naivety and some of the mistakes and social faux pas I have made along the way. That's fair enough. Some of it is genuinely laughable (some of it genuinely might reduce one to tears). But the upside is that I get to look at the industry in a different way. While many of the ideas of outsiders have been tried before and failed, occasionally, just occasionally, one idea gets through and starts to take hold.

In 2015 one such idea started to take root. My business partner Jeremy Harbour came up with an idea that at once seemed to make perfect sense to everyone we spoke to and at the same time was dismissed by almost everyone within the finance industry.

We had talked about this idea before. Jeremy and I wrote a bestselling book on it: *Agglomerate – Idea to IPO in 12 Months*,[1] but you might not have come across it before as it was written for small business owners, not for the sophisticated investor such as yourself. Our first job was not to convince small business owners that this idea made sense – they intuitively got it – but to convince them we could make it happen.

In the first section of this book, I explain the idea from the point of view of you, the investor. How it works,

---

1   Jeremy Harbour and Callum Laing, *Agglomerate – Idea to IPO in 12 Months* (Rethink Press Limited, 2016)

why it works, why others so far have struggled to replicate it despite its success. Why a great idea is no guarantee of success, and the mistake that cost us $250m!

Honestly, I would rather leave out that last bit, but people seem to take great pleasure in my pain, so I will share the gory details and what we learned from them. The things I do to entertain you!

I'm also going to share a case study of a company in the 1960s and 1970s that did one aspect of what we are doing exceptionally well and demonstrated the kind of returns that can be offered to those who take the time to understand the game that is being played.

In the second section of this book, I give an overview of the small business economy and why I believe this is literally a trillion-dollar opportunity. Not for us, but for you, the investor. Half the world's economy that was previously out of reach is suddenly up for grabs and wrapped up in a product that ticks seemingly every investor box.

Some of what I cover might even seem to be bordering on fluffy 'do good' nonsense but stick with it. I hope to show how you can exploit this opportunity for massive profits and still achieve a substantial net positive in the society in which we all live.

The second section takes what I propose in the first section to a whole new level. As Jeremy likes to say, 'This is the rocket fuel on the gasoline that is the TNT of this opportunity.'

Finally, in the third section of the book (don't worry, this is a light book, you can be back at your trading screens very quickly), I talk about how we put it all together and how you can profit from it – whether your investment horizons are twelve hours, twelve months or twelve years. If what you learned in the previous two sections showed you how to access a massive section of the economy that was completely off limits – where to dig for gold – the final section shows you how to profit from it today.

I make no claims to be an authority in the field of finance – far from it – but by having a foot in the camp of both small business and that of the world of investment and finance, perhaps I can provide a unique, or at least unusual, perspective on things. I hope you can use it to make massive returns and, as a side effect, create a lot of jobs for my small business peers!

Three circles: finally, a use for Venn diagrams!

The three sections of the book align with the diagram on the front cover, and my quest for the perfect investment opportunity. I started my entrepreneurial ventures as a kid selling homemade ice cream to local bars and restaurants in my neighbourhood. My career as an entrepreneur grew over time and as I became more successful, I started to have access to my own capital to become an investor in businesses myself. I discovered quickly, and painfully, that one of the traits that can make you a good entrepreneur – an unflinching belief that things will work out – is not necessarily a good trait as an investor.

However, as my approach to investing continued to evolve, I discovered that there were three areas, or circles, that investment opportunities tended to fall into. Over time, I realised that if an investment opportunity came to me that fell into just *one* of these circles then I was better off passing on it. If it fell into two of these circles, then it was definitely worth looking at. And if by some miracle the opportunity fell into all three circles, like a winning lottery ticket, it should be grabbed with both hands. Unfortunately, as I looked at the investing landscape around me, I realised that one out of three were everywhere you looked, two out of three existed but took some ferreting out, and three out of three were literally a golden ticket. If they existed at all, I couldn't find them. In fact, as it turns out, to find such opportunities we have to create them.

Those three circles are:

1. Liquidity – the ability to get in and out of an investment easily

2. Impact – the surety that any investment will make a difference / create jobs

3. Alpha – the likelihood of above-market returns

THE THREE-CIRCLE MODEL

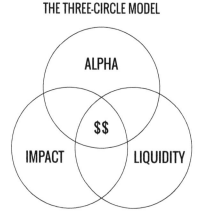

For me, this is the holy trinity of investing, but as simple as it looks, there is a nuance and a granularity to it.

Liquidity

The extremes of each of these circles, is a place to be avoided. In 'liquidity', if you follow it out to the edges you get the 'day traders' with zero regard for what value is being created or whether they can support a business. They will get in and out of a position in a day, or sometimes multiple times in a day, without caring whether the stock goes up or down. (This is not a criticism of traders, they play an important role in the ecosystem, but let's be careful to separate *trading* from *investing*.) Taken even further to the extremes of liquidity, you have the high frequency trading (HFT) that buys and sells in fractions of seconds, front-running your order (*Flashboys* by Michael Lewis explains this brilliantly).[2] In my experience, the further out you go the less the values and ethics have in common with those I try and teach my kids.

Impact

The extremes of 'impact' bring us to the well-meaning but often delusional entrepreneur who wants to 'save the world' but can't yet figure out how to create a sustainable enough business to pay their own wages. They are content to rail against the injustices of the world, occasionally even offering some solutions, but mostly failing to build a sustainable business model. And without that credibility, they are unable to gather any momentum for their 'passion project', thus probably reinforcing their own belief that the world is broken. Even the most well-meaning 'angel' investors fear to tread at the extremes of 'impact'. Sadly, it is the 'friends, family and fools' who get burnt at the far edge of this circle.

---

2   Michael Lewis, *Flashboys* (Penguin, 2015)

Alpha

The extremes of 'alpha' are well documented. Alpha is Wall Street speak for above-market returns, and of course it is on Wall Street that we see some of the worst excesses of chasing alpha without regard for others. Some enterprises are legal but unethical, such as sub-prime mortgages and the ratings agencies that enabled them. Others just blatantly cross the line, such as Bernie Madoff and his meticulously managed Ponzi scheme.

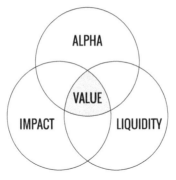

So, clearly playing at the extremes of these circles is not the way to go for an astute investor with a keen sense of right and wrong. The three sections of this book relate to the three circles in the diagram and I overlay them onto a weird phenomenon that seems to separate the finance world from half the economy. When things have always been done a certain way, it is often difficult to imagine them being done in any other way, but through the lens of these three circles, you too will be able to see this massive opportunity.

What I hope to show you is that seen through the intersection of these three circles, there is a massive opportunity waiting to be disrupted. However, before we explore that, we need to understand the environment that exists today.

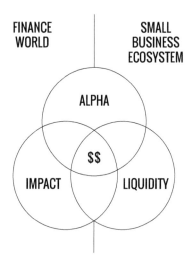

Three circles overlaying the intersection of finance versus the small economy

The business and finance paradox

While I have been an entrepreneur from a young age, hustling to make extra money, I was always fascinated by the finance world. I was at my most young and impressionable in the finance glory days of the early 1980s. Thatcher's Britain (or Reagan's US). Red braces, Filofaxes, sports cars and the birthing of 'yuppies' with the first mobile phone bricks. For a kid from a very poor background wanting to change his lot in life, it certainly held an intoxicating appeal, despite the fact that nobody in my world seemed to know what people in that world actually did.

The closest I ever got to being involved was a two-week 'work experience' at a Barclays Bank branch in Cambridge, England, where I grew up. Somehow removing paper clips from endless piles of duplicate paper in the back office while the 'bankers' whinged about their managers didn't light the same passion in me as I had expected when I told people I wanted to work in finance. But by then the glory days of the 1980s were long gone and I started to look elsewhere for my career aspirations.

Ten years later I was a little closer to the action when finance once again was heralded in the headlines of the news. This time I was working for an internet company at the height of the dot-com boom. Once again fortunes were being made – well, made *again* really. And this time, while I wasn't on Wall Street, I was working in the hottest sector and for one of the hottest companies. This company was one of the biggest internet service providers at the height of the internet boom. I had two fantastic years working for them (with six promotions in that time as I was the only geek who could communicate with management and clients), before setting out to start my own recruitment company in the telco/IP space. Life was good and while the term 'yuppie' had faded, I would have embraced it nicely with its commensurate trappings of wealth and excess (and the not altogether healthy lifestyle to go with it!).

Once again, the music stopped. The bubble burst. The weekend trips to New York dried up, the fancy apartments in Amsterdam and Dublin were returned, and I settled back into trying to figure out how to build a more sustainable business and life for myself. I also took the opportunity to move to Asia. Even twenty years ago it was clear that one of the biggest macro trends affecting the planet was the largest transfer of wealth in history from west to east. As a young entrepreneur, it definitely seemed to make sense to be on the receiving end of that equation, not the giving end.

Yet even being based in one of the most exciting and fast-growing regions of the world as I tried to figure out how to build better businesses, there was always this weird conundrum I could never get my head around that went back to my interest in the finance industry. How was it that the world was so obsessed with finance and investment and yet it bore absolutely zero correlation to the world of small business, which when I looked around seemed to be everywhere? The effect of interest rates, the price of oil, what the FTSE or the S&P had done on a given day all seemed to be hugely important to the world given the column inches and talking heads dedicated to these drivers. And yet, as far as I could tell, they had next to zero effect on my business or the other small businesses around me. How was it that everywhere I looked there were small businesses thriving, struggling, growing, shrinking, and yet while you might hear the odd politician wax lyrical about small business, the news was filled with stories about the economy, the markets and the latest catastrophe that the biggest companies of the day were inflicting on the planet. Nobody was talking about the world of small business.

In *The Snowball*, Warren Buffett's book,[3] he explains that one of his biggest challenges is that he needs to invest $100m a week, every week, for Berkshire Hathaway to be successful. And there are just not that many companies out there that can absorb that much money. The poor man, my heart went out to him. Fifteen years ago, sitting in my office, I definitely couldn't help him out with that $100m, but I certainly could have relieved him of, say, $2m. This was not some risky speculative punt. It was one of our biggest clients, saying they could double our revenue and triple our profits that year if we could take on this project they wanted to give us.

---

3   Warren Buffett, *The Snowball* (Bloomsbury, 2009)

I could put that $2m to work, and work quickly (just a side note for any day traders, 'quickly' in the small business world might mean one or two years – but I was confident I could double Warren's money for him in that sort of time frame).

How was it so hard to connect the money that needed a home with the people who needed it? That question was too big for me at the time and so I filed it away in the 'life's mysteries' cabinet and got back on the phone to my client to explain that I didn't have the resources to take on their project, they would have to give it to someone else.

I was no different from any other small business owner out there. While it was frustrating that there was no access to capital, perhaps we didn't have the intellectual capacity to give it more than a fleeting thought. There was rent to be paid, there were clients to be serviced, staff to be soothed and a myriad other more urgent issues to be addressed.

Yet step back from that and you see a more systematic problem. Half the world's gross domestic product (GDP) is created by small businesses. Approximately 90% of private sector employment comes from small businesses. And yet, those Masters of the Universe I so envied on Wall Street have no 'product' which allows them to tap into and profit from small business.

Many years later, I was on the phone to fellow entrepreneur Jeremy Harbour, and he started telling me about something he was thinking about and a completely unique way of addressing a problem that faced most successful small businesses. This wouldn't quite solve the conundrum of how to get Warren's capital into the hands of small business, but it was certainly revolutionary and seemed to solve many of the problems I and my fellow small business owners faced. A few months later, we started working together as partners at Unity Group and 'Project Roll Up' began.

'Project Roll Up' became 'Agglomeration™' – the new name for the business model, which I base a case study on later. As we started to stress test it and develop it, it became obvious that this was something that could potentially be the first very important step in reconnecting the capital markets with the small businesses that created the value.

Ultimately, it would result in the creation of hundreds of millions of dollars of value, kick us both in the teeth a few times and set us on a path that we believe is a trillion-dollar opportunity and rich pickings for you, the smarter than average investor.

SECTION ONE

LIQUIDITY

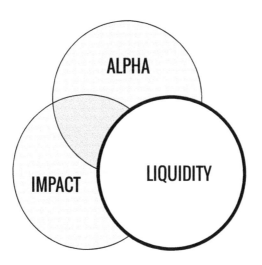

Liquidity describes the degree to which an asset or security can be quickly bought or sold in the market at a price reflecting its intrinsic value.

Agglomeration™

agglomerate. v. 1680s, from Latin agglomeratus, past participle of agglomerare 'to wind or add onto a ball', from ad- 'to' (see ad-) + glomerare 'wind up in a ball', from glomus (genitive glomeris) 'ball of yarn', from PIE root *glem-. Related: agglomerated; agglomerating.
    — etymonline.com

Simply put, an agglomeration is a publicly listed holding company with a buy and hold strategy focused on small- to medium-sized enterprises (SMEs) across multiple industries and geographies. All the companies become fully owned subsidiaries and their owners become joint owners of the bigger entity as they are compensated with locked-up stock in the holding company. No cash. The companies are allowed to maintain their independence and their compensation is based on their profit contribution to the holding company over time.

Companies are only acquired for low multiples that are earnings per share accretive to more than offset the dilutionary effect of issuing more stock. This approach maximises the considerable arbitrage between small business valuations and big public company valuations. It creates the ultimate in decentralised, entrepreneurial organisations with a highly incentivised and motivated leadership team.

From an investment perspective, assuming the board executes the agglomeration strategy successfully, this holding company should offer you, the investor, an incredibly fast-growth, low-risk, high-dividend-yielding stock.

In this section, I will share with you how an Agglomeration™ works and more importantly why it works for investors. It is impossible to do that without explaining why a small business owner would agree to give up ownership of their life's work to be a part of this and so I will briefly explain that. If you would like to understand the mindset of small business owners better, then I recommend our last book *Agglomerate* –

Idea to IPO in 12 Months which was written for the business owner.

After that I will drill into some of the features of this model that can make it attractive to own.

Drawing from history: Rockefeller did it first!

In 1872, John D Rockefeller was also thinking about grouping companies together. In the burgeoning oil business, Rockefeller had worked out he could get vastly discounted transportation of his oil if he committed to buying whole trains up at a time. Yet he didn't have the volume of oil himself to fill a whole train, so he started looking at the industry and his competitors. Rockefeller proceeded to buy up those competitors using the stock in his own company, Standard Oil, as compensation. For him the actual quality of the businesses he was buying was less important than the fact he could now use their volume in order to get the discounts on the transport he so needed.

Now, to be clear, Rockefeller had other designs on this group of companies he was busy building. His objective was to build a cartel, increase prices and basically end up with a monopoly (none of which was illegal in those times).

Cartels were nothing new, but they were famously hard to manage. Of course, the basic idea is that everyone signs up to keep their prices above a certain rate, but it only takes one unscrupulous or desperate member to reduce their prices for side deals and the cartel starts to crumble. Rockefeller's shrewdness was to tie the fortunes of all to each other. Additionally, he also used his new-found powers to make it incredibly hard for anyone on the outside to compete. In fact, the deal he struck with the railroads was such that competitors could still use the trains, but the rebates for volume would only go to the cartel members. Hence the more volume the competitors put through, the more profitable the game for those in the cartel. Smart cookie that Rockefeller.

Agglomeration™ is not nearly as nefarious or anti-competitive as Rockefeller was but it is clear that there are many advantages to small businesses of being part of a group with a vested interest in your success, plus the bargaining power that can potentially come through the consolidation of interests.

The Agglomeration™ business model centres on the creation of a publicly listed company that allows great small businesses to swap their private stock for public stock yet keep full control of their own entities.

The value for investors of holding Agglomeration™ stock comes primarily from the arbitrage between the price small private businesses can be acquired for and the price big public companies trade for. Using 'expensive' stock to acquire lower-priced stock is nothing new.

More recently than Rockefeller's nineteenth-century innovation, we can see an even closer model to Agglomeration™ by Henry Singleton in the form of the Teledyne company. Teledyne was a conglomerate that performed 130 acquisitions in the 1960s, about thirteen a year. To do this, Singleton predominantly used his valuable stock and a combination of debt. He would acquire the companies, often below twelve times earnings when his own shares were trading at around twenty-five times. In short, for every dollar of earnings he was acquiring, he was creating more than $13 of value for the existing shareholders. Between 1961 and 1971, his earnings grew a staggering 566 times alongside a commensurate growth in stock. In that decade his earnings per share (EPS) went from $0.13 to $8.55.[4]

Needless to say, this level of growth came with the volatility you would expect, but Singleton remained focused on the EPS and the cashflow of the business, and shareholders who stuck with him were amply rewarded – in bull markets and bear, as we will come back to later in Section Three.

---

4   The Investor's Field Guide, 'Shrinkage vs. Growth' (2019), http://investorfieldguide.com/shrinkage-vs-growth

The Agglomeration™ model works because small business owners are prepared to swap their privately owned shares for publicly owned shares at a considerably lower multiple than the multiple the PLC is trading at. They are also swapping their shares for an initial consideration that is likely less than they would receive if they were selling on the open market. And yet they are queuing up to do so. Unity Group, our office in Singapore, receives around 1,000 requests a year from companies looking to join this model.

To an entrepreneur, the appeal of this solution rarely needs selling. It solves many problems for them, although interestingly the 'main' problem it solves varies from owner to owner. To someone who has never been a small business owner it may seem to beggar belief that any rational business owner would consider this solution and give up ownership of their business for such a relatively low upfront payment in stock.

Recently, I was presenting to a group of investors over lunch and a heated argument kicked off at the table after I had finished speaking. On one side was a high net worth (HNW) individual who had built and sold businesses. On the other side was someone who had never built a business but had done scores of deals in private equity (PE) and investment banking. The HNW guy thought the model was brilliant, the PE guy thought we were flat out lying and it couldn't possibly work. I rarely see much value in trying to convince someone through argument, but I was happy to enjoy my coffee while the two of them fought it out. It was a discussion I've had many times, but it was nice to have someone else arguing the case for me.

On the traditional finance side, the arguments follow the same basic format.

No rational business owner would 'sell' their business for below market rates. There's no way they wouldn't want cash upfront. Why would they trust us? Why would they trust the other business owners? Why would we trust them? Wouldn't they just take the shares and let their business crumble? And if they were stupid enough to give us their business, why wouldn't we hire some MBAs to go in and make their business better? Why would we leave them in charge?

All valid arguments if you are used to buying companies that are worth $100–$200m or above, which is the world most PE guys operate in (although I'm not convinced PE is doing such a great job with its current way of thinking with those bigger companies either). However, in the world in which we operate, our small businesses are in the $1–10m range – too small for most PE. Plus, as entrepreneurs ourselves we come at it from a very different angle. We didn't ask, 'How do we make money out of this sector?' We asked, 'How do we solve problems for ourselves and our peers?' And as it turned out, solving those problems makes a lot of money. Or more specifically, unlocks a lot of latent value for the business owners and investors in the stock.

So why would a small business owner act 'irrationally' and swap 100% of their privately owned shares for locked-up shares in a PLC they don't have full control over?

The first thing to understand is that this isn't a 'sale' in the conventional sense of the word. The business owners we work with still want to grow their business and they realise they can grow it more effectively as part of a PLC than they can as a private entity. If it was a sale, you could talk about valuation in the conventional sense, but how do you place a value on something you don't want to sell? There is no linguistic terminology in the English language that I'm aware of for that set-up. In the absence of this, we have to use the word 'valuation', but it is already misleading. Perhaps another way to look at it is they are joining an incubator or a bootcamp to help them grow. Either way, the deal is structured as a perpetual 'earn-in' for the business owner. The more profit they contribute to the group, the more shares they are rewarded with. Broadly speaking, they get three times the incremental profit they contribute to the group. In the first year they also get whatever is on their balance sheet.

So, for a company that joins the group having done $1m in ebit (earnings before interest and taxes) the previous year (our entry point for the size of companies we are looking for), they might end up with, say, $4m in stock on day one. In the first year with us, if they did $1.25m, that extra $250k profit contribution to the group would be multiplied by three and we would give them another $750k of shares. If the following year they did $1.75m, they would be issued another $1.5m of stock (three times the $500k uplift). All told, after three years, they would be sitting on $6.25m in stock. And that is assuming that the share price stayed flat during that time. This incentive scheme is ongoing, they are on a perpetual earn-in. The more they contribute, the more they earn.

Of course, this is a little bit of clever semantics. They would have to be growing to get that, but isn't that how most deals are structured? The only difference is that instead of telling people they will get six times (or more) based on hitting targets, we underplay it. The other options in the market, such as a trade sale, may shout about buying at a higher multiple, but this is always predicated on hitting targets and for numerous reasons it rarely works out for the business owner.

But business owners that have built companies generating $1m in ebit or more are not dumb: they can work out the maths of our model and have faith that they will be able to grow their business more effectively as part of a PLC than on their own.

But interestingly, the 'price' at which we acquire companies, while important, is rarely the main reason they want to join our model. Small business owners face a 'scale paradox' that manifests itself in many ways and it means that they often reach a certain size and then plateau. And plateauing for a business owner is almost as bad as going backwards.

For example, procurement best practice of big companies is never to give big contracts to small companies. Consequently, big companies give big contracts to other big companies who often turn around and outsource them to the smaller companies who are better at delivering, but they will cream off the bulk of the profits in the process.

At exactly the time when the small business needs to attract a good senior team to help them grow, that talent deems working for a small business too risky and so goes to the big corporates with the better incentives. It is nearly impossible for small businesses to win the talent war.

And of course, small businesses don't have access to capital to grow. While a big company can get a loan from a bank or issue a bond, that is sadly off the table for small businesses.

Other reasons business owners have cited for wanting to join this model also include wanting to be a part of something bigger. It is a lonely job at the top, and so joining a group of other successful, like-minded business owners who now have a vested interest in your success is very attractive. We have had other business owners who were going to take their company public themselves but realised that by joining us they would avoid some of the scrutiny they would receive on their own. For example, the founder's net worth becomes very public if they list themselves. They may also not want their clients to have the full transparency that they would have. A big client would be able to see exactly how much revenue they contribute, which makes future negotiations that much harder.

At the end of the day, the important point for you as an investor to know and for the model to work is not whether the investment community understands why small businesses choose to join it, but that they *do* regularly join it, which is easily demonstrable.

So beyond why they join, what else is important for an investor to know about the Agglomeration™ model? Let's break it down into liquidity and returns, as these generate the most common questions: can I get in and out of the stock easily and what are my expected returns?

Let's start with returns.

Returns

How does an Agglomeration™ provide returns? There are three key ways:

1. Accretive acquisitions

2. Organic growth (of the subsidiary companies)

3. Synergies

Accretive acquisitions

The best due diligence you can do is the price you pay.
— Attributed to Warren Buffett

This is clearly the foundation of the Agglomeration™ model and as long as we can continue to acquire companies with stock at a multiple that is below what we are trading, the value for existing shareholders, measured in EPS, should grow significantly. For a typical Agglomeration™, we would be looking to add around fifteen to twenty new acquisitions a year, although the expectation is that would grow year on year. That's fifteen to twenty *new* major acquisitions, but our expectation is that many of the existing companies are also expected to engage in their own acquisitions.

The minimum ebit requirement of a company joining is $1m, so an Agglomeration™ should be able to grow its ebit from zero to at least $20m in the first year or so. Pretty healthy growth. There are a few other key variables to understand in this model. For ease of maths, let's assume the company joining is doing $1m of ebit. The PLC pays $5m in stock up-front for that business: the difference between what the business owner receives and what the PLC pays includes things like Unity Group's fees, legal fees, any cash off the table, introducers' fees and so on. If the PLC is trading at fifteen times price to earnings (P/E), which is not unusual for a big PLC, then in that one transaction we have created $10m of value for existing shareholders (the difference between buying $1m at five times and trading at fifteen times). Do that twenty times in a year and you have created $200m of value. Or, more accurately, you have *unlocked* it. The value has always been in these small businesses, they have just been too illiquid for you, the investor, to access. If creating shares to buy profit is still confusing you, for now, just be aware that it works and is widely used by companies who are doing M&A and in most but not all cases it is the preferred currency for carrying out acquisitions.

Remember the argument between the PE guy and the HNW? One of the questions the PE wanted answering was: 'Why wouldn't a business owner get their shares and run off and leave their business to perish?' (As you can see, some finance guys have a very dim view of entrepreneurs!) Our answer was that someone who has poured ten to twenty years of their life into their business and has a massive earn-in potential is not likely to walk away from the business just to pull one over on us. But since the question kept coming up, what we did do was introduce a way to completely 'de-risk' it for investors. Now, every single company we acquire needs to achieve 80% of their previous year's ebit in their first year with us, otherwise we reserve the right to unwind the deal. In effect, they would give back their shares (still locked) and we would return their business. Since the companies remain independent when they join us, this is very easy to achieve and basically renders every acquisition risk-free for the existing shareholders. In fact, because we are acquiring these companies at such a low upfront multiple, we calculated that 50% of the companies could go bust in their second year with us and it would still be EPS accretive. Fortunately, debt-free, decades-old, profitable businesses don't tend to go bust overnight!

Organic growth

Interestingly enough, our model is not dependent on the growth of the companies in the group. Of course we want them to grow, but unlike a PE or venture capital (VC) model we are not dependent on one of our portfolio becoming a 'unicorn' to recoup the risk of the others not performing. The problem with that model is that it puts enormous pressure on subsidiaries to over-expand, and the number one killer of small businesses is over-expansion. In the VC world you just factor those failures into your model and double down on the pressure for your remaining companies to expand.

With our model, there is a big incentive for them to grow (the bonus shares) but there is no penalty if they don't. The reality of small business is that its revenues and profits can fluctuate greatly. Our model works regardless, and by and large we expect to be about breaking even each year. Some companies will do well, others not so well, but as with any portfolio, our risk is limited and of course we can still grow substantially via acquisition. For us, a company that grows at a nice steady clip and spits off cashflow is much more attractive than one that could over-reach and fall over.

Having said all that, one of the reasons that small businesses join an Agglomeration™ is that they want to grow and should be able to do that more effectively as part of the group.

We have seen companies land contracts that were ten times the size of any previous contract, just by nature of the fact they were pitching for it as a PLC rather than a small independent. Then there is the ability to attract and retain key members of staff. As noted above, this is an area in which many small businesses often lose the talent war to big companies. Finally, although it is not exactly 'organic', many of the companies that join an Agglomeration™ are now looking to do their own acquisitions. Maybe there are competitors they have had their eyes on, or maybe they have some suppliers that they would like to acquire and bring on board.

So, although the model doesn't depend on it, we very much believe that our subsidiary companies can grow much more effectively as part of a group than on their own.

Synergies

I have deliberately put synergies third in this list as we believe it is the least likely to drive value and yet it is the one the finance industry talks about the most. While there are obvious synergies between some of the companies in the group, we have learned over time and through trial and error that although synergies look fantastic on paper, they very rarely work out as you anticipate in real life. What does work well is the sharing of best practice, contacts and so on, and that goes on. We get all the principals of the subsidiaries together twice a year, plus they all communicate through an online platform, and it makes sense for them to help each other where they can.

So those are the three main drivers of return for investors. Let's now look at liquidity before we explore what can go wrong.

Liquidity

Although *liquidity* in their stock is not always the main reason why business owners want to join an Agglomeration™, without it I'm not sure the others would be nearly as valuable. You have to remember that a typical small business owner has zero liquidity in their business. Even if they were able to find an investor who would put money in, that investor would understandably want the money to go into the business, not out to the owner.

What drives liquidity?

News and scale are two of the biggest drivers of liquidity in stock. And they are the two things that most listed micro and small caps (stocks typically with a market cap below $500m and $2bn) are unable to offer. Fortunately, we are strong in both these areas, plus we have a communication strategy that rivals most big PLCs.

News. With an Agglomeration™ aiming to complete one to two acquisitions per month, you are hard pressed to see a month go by when you don't make a material announcement to the market – and each of those announcements need to be shareholder positive. Additionally, when you are dealing with a portfolio of companies, there is always something going on that can be talked about, whether it is a big new client or a new senior hire.

Scale. The other significant advantage that an Agglomeration™ has over a typical micro or small cap is that the board is not involved in the day-to-day running of the individual companies. The CEO of the group should be able to devote all his or her time to communicating with investors, the media, speaking at conferences and so forth. This is a far cry from the average small company that goes public, where the CEO has zero interaction with the market after the initial fund-raise because they are so busy trying to deal with staff and clients.

So – what can go wrong?

It all sounds pretty great, right? But a great strategy doesn't always lead to a great result.

In 2016 we put all the theories to the test and built our first Agglomeration™. Eighteen months later, I wrote an article on the experience and the lessons learned. I base the following case study on this article.[5]

CASE STUDY: THE MARKETING GROUP PLC – LESSONS LEARNT FROM LOSING $250M

In business it is often said that any decision is better than none. Even a bad decision can move you forward. It's probably a good theory, but some decisions can be really, really expensive. One specific decision we made ended up knocking $250m off the market capital of our business and nearly cost us everything we had.

The idea

In 2015, our little company started working on a project that we believed, and still believe, would change the landscape for small businesses around the world and enable them to compete with the big boys, win bigger contracts, hire more senior people and reward those who create the most value. As outlined

---

5   Callum Laing, 'Lessons learnt from losing $250m ...', *The Asian Entrepreneur* (2017), www.asianentrepreneur.org/lessons-learnt-losing-250m. Some edits have been made to the original message to accommodate the case study within this publication. Original article available at the link above.

earlier, the idea, which we called 'Agglomeration™', was to create a publicly listed company and allow great small businesses to swap their private stock for public stock yet keep full control of their own entities – a collaborative IPO (initial public offering) but leaving the entrepreneurs in charge and incentivised to build their business.

We knew it would be tough to get it up and running. It was. We thought once it was up and running it would be much easier. It wasn't.

The glory days

After many false starts, we finally managed to get the company listed. What came next over the following quarter was pretty exceptional. As we announced deal after deal, bringing in great companies to the group, the model snowballed in front of our eyes. On the one hand, the share price soared as investors clamoured to get hold of the relatively small amount of free-floating stock. On the other hand, more and more companies were knocking on our door wanting to join the group, and with every deal we announced, more people wanted the stock. At the same time, we were also dealing with a flurry of media requests, speaking requests, people wanting to work for us, people wanting to sell us stuff and institutions wanting to talk about giving us money.

If I was to pick a moment from this time it was when Nasdaq invited us to their HQ in Times Square, New York, and put our names up outside on a five-storey digital screen, all while we were being filmed by a documentary crew.

Those were heady times, no doubt, but the growth was putting a huge financial strain on us. While we were keen to keep bringing in more great companies and announce more great deals, we were looking at a shortfall of tens of millions of dollars to do it.

Despite the fact our little business had soared past a $100m market cap and then a month later $200m, banks were, understandably, nervous about loaning money to a company before it had published its full first yearly results. Fortunately, or not as it would turn out, there was no shortage of other financial institutions who were more than happy to loan us money against the value of our personal shares. This is a widely known practice. Unfortunately, as we would later learn, it is also well known to some of its more shady operators. However, someone we trusted recommended an institution in the USA and having met with them a couple of times we decided to go ahead with a leverage deal.

They would 'hold' three million of our personal shares (valued at the time at €24m) and in return would loan us €9m which we could use to close a couple of the deals we were in late stage discussions with. At the end of two years, we would give them back the €9m plus interest and they would give us back the shares. All pretty straightforward.

The mistakes

In retrospect, while we got a lot of things right, we also got a few things wrong. Our lack of experience in the public markets, a very junior and inexperienced team on the ground and a constant firehose of opportunities, criticisms, congratulations and conflicting advice were not conducive to over-delivering to our various stakeholders. The fact that our whole team had been working seven-day weeks in the run up to the IPO and then moved to working days and nights in the post-IPO period, doing the acquisitions, didn't help anyone either. Sleep deprivation is not a good state in which to make healthy decisions.

Sometimes we communicated too much to the market (sorry Nasdaq!), other times not enough. We did deals that, looking back, weren't as smart as they seemed. Our contracts weren't always up to scratch and often required multiple drafts, and our faith in others was unrealistic. We threw money at problems that would have been better ignored and ignored problems that would turn out to be critical. And we had a constant stream of people coming in to 'advise' us on everything we did.

While it would be easy to point fingers at those 'professional' advisers, the reality is that, like many things in life, we were getting diametrically opposing advice from advisers on almost every topic. Our mistake, which we own 100%, was choosing to listen to those who told us what we wanted to hear and ignore the rest.

Yet often the only way you can tell the difference is through experience. And the way you get that experience? Mistakes ...

The 'alleged' crime

Back in the craziness of that first ninety days we had completed the deal with the US-based institution, the money had been promised and consequently we were able to announce a couple more great acquisitions that would be joining the group. The pace of activity was no less frenetic, and we were desperately trying to staff-up to cope with demand.

However, behind the scenes something wasn't quite right with the share price. Having gone up like a skyrocket, we were well prepared for people 'taking their wins' and selling off. Sure enough, many people did just that, having made, in some cases, 700 or 800% returns on their investments, but it seemed like something more sinister was at play.

Our retail investors were crying foul. Someone had a massive sell order in the market and appeared to be deliberately driving the share price down. At first, we dismissed it, but as the share price continued to tumble each day we launched an investigation. The obvious first stop was the institution we had just sent three million shares to, but they were contractually obliged not to touch those shares. They even sent us a screenshot of the account in a third party's hands to show us the shares were safe.

The impact on our business was very real and I remember those days as some of the most stressful, and sleepless, I have ever been through. There were only two options. One was the investment bank we were using, but after accusing them the MD immediately flew out to Singapore to explain to us in person why that would never happen. The other option was one or more of the entrepreneurs in the group, but they were all locked up and so didn't even have the power to sell shares.

Despite living in a world of real-time updates, in Europe, where our stock was listed, you have to wait one month before EuroClear will give you a breakdown of who is holding your stock (not the individual accounts, just the banks). Blockchain couldn't come fast enough, but over two months it became clear that despite their denials, the institution that was supposedly holding our stock in escrow had actually been dumping it in the market.

Needless to say, they also weren't providing us with the cash they promised ...

(The use of the word 'alleged' in relation to the crime and other softeners is on advice pending further legal action.)

The unravelling

The Agglomeration™ model was made as robust as we could make it. The companies we worked with carried no debt, they were all profitable, and were run by good entrepreneurs who had worked hard to deliver value to their clients. We weren't betting on start-ups and we weren't betting that these companies would over-deliver in the future, just that they would stay about the same. The companies were also diversified over different niches and territories so as best to protect the wealth of the group.

Yet despite the resilient nature of the model, there are few PLCs out there who can withstand an onslaught like the one we were currently under. With three million unauthorised shares flooding the market, the share price went into freefall. Even our most loyal investors got spooked and wanted out before they lost all their gains.

While we had concern for our investors, our primary concern was for the founders who had joined (who also represented the biggest investor base). Unfortunately, as the stock continued to tank, several of the later-joining companies decided to back out of the deal. This was supposed to be a collaborative IPO so if they wanted to exit, we weren't going to force them to stay, yet the knock-on effect to the remaining businesses was like a kick in the guts.

As the market saw deals unravelling, that put ever more downward pressure on the stock price and consequently our pipeline of future deals began to dissolve in front of our eyes. Under this sort of pressure, more mistakes crept in. Announcements were rushed through to the market that arguably should never have been made. Desperate attempts to rustle up more cash and shares for existing founders often led to more problems than solutions. Our own efforts to show support for the stock by investing more were even seen by some as 'profiteering'.

As the year came to an end there was one bit of advice that was coming through loud and clear. We needed to step down from the board and bring in other professionals to restore investor confidence.

The pain

As 2017 started, it was quite clear that we were still a long way from turning the corner. We removed ourselves from the board and bought in decades of experience whose job it was to try and restore the faith of the battered investors and the founders of the group who still believed in the model, knew their companies were good, and couldn't understand how the group was so undervalued. Their first step was to try to 'rip off the bandaid' and get all the bad news out in one go, so that they could then rebuild from the bottom up.

Eighteen months after it listed, The Marketing Group (TMG.ST) is charting a different path. Rejecting the Agglomeration™ model, it is currently focused on organic growth and product innovation.

As for the alleged crime? We have spent a large amount of time and money chasing this so far. Because of the international nature of white-collar crime, it is very difficult to find support to pursue such dealings and the potential cost of doing so could be hundreds of thousands of dollars. While morally it might be the right thing to do, it would never recover the damage that has been done.

When we talk about a $250m loss of market capitalisation it is a pretty abstract concept to most. Such losses might seem victimless, but each one of those dollars has a story behind it. We got to hear those stories every single day. In many cases it was our friends, families and colleagues who suffered when the share price tanked. The cumulative amount of loss might seem abstract, but to the individuals who owned the stock, it was very real.

Although many people suffered from the results of that one act, it was ultimately our responsibility to have created that wealth and it was our responsibility when it was destroyed again. Had this been a one-off, it would have been easy to walk away, but we never approached this as a one-time deal. The reason we were doing this work was because we genuinely believed that small businesses deserve a fair shake of the stick. As painful, and as ultimately expensive, as TMG became, what kept us going, and having conversations with disappointed founders, angry investors and confused staff, day after day, was that we still had faith in the idea.

The lessons

For Unity Group, our little company that put this together and has fought for it harder than anyone, we took two key lessons to guide us in the future. The first is 'funding' related, the second is 'everything else'.

Funding

The start of all our problems came through a lack of funding and the decision to trust someone who, at best, didn't act with integrity and in the spirit of our business or business model to get access to capital. We were naive about the costs involved and in all future agglomerations we will be raising plenty of capital in the markets so that we have a war chest for the future. Raising money for small businesses is nearly impossible, but for decent-sized PLCs it is relatively easy. We now have a board of advisers that includes some of the brightest in Wall Street and the City of London. While we believed we were rigorous in our dealings before, we were too trusting – a mistake we won't repeat.

Everything else

There is no doubt we made mistakes the first time around. However, as we swelled the ranks of our internal team, we brought in many very talented managers who rewrote contracts, improved the due diligence process and set standards and procedures for communications. The model itself has evolved through time as we've learned what works and what doesn't. There are subtle but important changes to the order in which we do things that will prevent, or at least mitigate against, 'black swan' events.

Our model was put under the most extreme pressure we could ever have imagined and while it wasn't pretty, we still have a group of great small businesses that are working well together, winning big contracts and recruiting senior staff. The model itself is resilient but, like any innovation, it gets sharper and better on the grindstone of the market.

The future

Any invention, innovation or new product is normally a poor imitation of the final solution it becomes. We learned from the companies we worked with and more from those that wouldn't work with us. We learned from our investors and again from the investors who wouldn't work with us. And we learned about ourselves and our team, what our capabilities were and what areas were best left to others.

The problems facing good, well-run small businesses remain the same and Agglomeration™ remains the best model we know of to help solve those problems. The markets will change, our model will adapt, but fundamentally we are here to help small businesses scale more effectively. The impact on them, their teams, their clients and the greater economy can be game-changing for all involved.

The price we paid for being too trusting cost us $250m in market capitalisation, but it actually cost us far more in opportunity. It was an expensive lesson. However, the real cost would be far higher if we didn't learn from it and push forward to continue what we started.

Every small business we work with has been through its own version of this rollercoaster and the best come out the other side stronger and more determined than ever. We are lucky enough to be able to work with those businesses, compare war stories and then push forward using everything we have learned to take them to the next level.

And that is the most important business decision we can make.

Lessons learned: 2020

So, was it a bad idea? While we gave that question a lot of thought at the time, the reality is that even some of the best good ideas don't work. Not because they are not good ideas, but because good ideas don't exist in a vacuum. They need great people, great execution and a fair dollop of luck to come out the other side and reach a point where everyone believes it was always obvious.

For us, despite the painful setback, we were absolutely convinced that the idea was right. Mistakes had been made and fortune hadn't been kind, but we were pretty sure that a relentless focus on connecting investors and great small business owners with a product that supported the needs of both would eventually seem like an obvious idea.

Like all business owners, we were familiar with setbacks (albeit not quite at this scale!) and we took our time to learn the lessons, make things right with those who had been hurt and then get back on the horse and press forward.

Volatility: the price you pay for ownership

> If you want stability, buy a bond. If you want above-market returns, volatility is the price you pay.
> — Morgan Housel, Collaborative Fund

Call it a bug in the Agglomeration™ model, call it a feature or call it the price you pay. Whatever you call it, volatility – a share price that swings wildly – is inherent in the Agglomeration™ model – at least it was in the early days.

Given the bulk of the shares are locked up (because the majority of shares are owned by the business/subsidiary owners) there is a relatively small amount of free trading shares. That means that on any given day, one person, or a small group of people deciding to buy or sell, can have a dramatic effect on the share price.

Is this a bad thing? Well, it can be unnerving to see swings of 20% or more on any given day but you need to pick your metric. If you want a perfectly stable share price, there are plenty of illiquid stocks out there that won't budge at all. As soon as you introduce buyers and sellers that will change. Because the nature of the Agglomeration™ model is to be making regular material announcements to the market, this also drives buyers into the stock. I can talk all I like about wanting to find good, patient investors who will sit and hold their stock for years and happily enjoy its appreciation and the healthy dividends. But the reality is that traders also love this stock. Volatility is where they make their money and any stock with wild swings is great for them. Plus, the constant flow of news that we put out, normally a material announcement about another acquisition, keeps them on their toes. And of course, you make money in the market by trying to predict what comes next. If a PLC is announcing accretive acquisitions each month and that tends to boost the share price, then there is money to be made for the trader by trying to guess the timing of the next announcement. Unfortunately, less ethically, there is money to be made by spreading false rumours, good or bad, on internet forums.

A great example of this, illustrated wonderfully by Ben Carlson, is the tale of Amazon stock.[6] As the talking heads are wont to do from time to time, they trot out the old line of if you had just bought $10,000 of Amazon stock at IPO time, it would now be worth nearly $10 million. What they neglect to mention is that several times during that journey the value of your stock would have fallen off a cliff. Around the time of the dot-com crash for example, would you have held onto your stock when it fell 20%? What about when it fell 40%? Could you sell now and still walk away with half a million dollars of profit from your initial $10k? No? Going to hold? Good choice, a few months later it's back up to where it was before. You're now sitting on a cool million-dollar profit, but now it's in freefall again. Time to cash in or are you holding off for better times? It's now down 60%. Ready to sell? Down 80%. You can still lock in enough profit to buy a house. Or are you going to follow it all the way down? The newspapers and analysts are suggesting the company is unlikely to survive the year. You're still a believer? It's now down 95% from the peak.

What does everyone else know that you don't? Technically you're still up, but it doesn't feel like that. Human emotion is such that it feels like someone just stole a million dollars out of your bank. If you were

---

6   Ben Carlson, 'How to Win Any Argument About the Stock Market', *Fortune* (2019), https://fortune.com/2019/06/11/stock-market-how-to-win-arguments

willing to hold through such enormous drawdowns, such crazy volatility, you were either dumb, a visionary or you had the constitution of Warren Buffett. But Buffett is one of the wealthiest men in the world because he has a unique ability to turn off some of those human emotions, such as fear, and instead bets against them.

I freely admit, I didn't have the stomach for it in those days. I bought Amazon fairly near the first peak and sold out at a loss, long before it reached its bottom.

Over time, averaged out, the stock market goes up a fairly steady 10% a year. We have to believe that over time the market will fairly value our stock, but in the short term, emotion and trends are what drive it, and not only do we have no control over either, it is an inevitability for any stock that is going to be fast growth.

Even if we look at the Amazon stock in recent times, as one of the most heavily traded stocks, its volatility in a single year is incredible. Between March 2018 and March 2019, the price has gone from above $2,000 down to below $1,400 and back up again.

Another classic along these lines is the story that comes out every few years about Apple. If you had just bought Apple stock instead of buying those products. If you had invested $2,495 in Apple stock instead of the very first Apple Macintosh in January 1984, then, as Yaron Yitzhak details,[7] that investment today would have increased 38,500% to be worth $960,000 (as of June 2019).

Oh, how silly we are for buying products instead of stocks! Yet let's look at two other points of time in Apple's stock history. Nine months before the launch of the Apple Mac, in April 1983, the shares were trading at $52. Twenty years later, April 2003, guess what the shares were trading at? $52.[8] I'm not sure that if you had invested in Apple stock rather than an Apple computer, you would have been feeling that clever.

The beauty of investing is that on a long or short enough timeline you can prove pretty much anything!

Robert Shiller, in his book *Irrational Exuberance*,[9] posits that volatility is twenty times higher on a public company's equity than on the underlying fundamentals. That makes sense: very little changes that much on a day-to-day basis in business, and yet a single fund manager choosing to go in, or come out, of a stock

---

7   Yaron Yitzhak, 'This is how rich you'd be if you bought Apple stock instead of its products', *the next web* (2019), https://thenextweb.com/plugged/2019/06/18/this-is-how-rich-youd-be-if-you-bought-apple-stock-instead-of-its-products
8   Macrotrends, www.macrotrends.net/stocks/charts/AAPL/apple/stock-price-history
9   Robert J Shiller, *Irrational Exuberance: Revised and Expanded Third Edition* (Princeton University Press, 2016)

can make a huge difference to the price and thus the volatility.

Is this a problem for us? Well, if the share price goes too low, we need to employ bonds or other strategies to keep doing acquisitions. When it goes too high, it causes suspicion among the inbound companies. They know they are likely to swap at one price, but that the price will likely return to the mean at some point in the future. Our only answer is to focus on the long term, not the short term, and concentrate on what we can control, not worry about what we cannot.

Controlling liquidity

Over time, volatility in an Agglomeration™ stock should get less. The reason is that as the founders' lock-ups end, they will start to sell down small percentages of their ownership, putting more volume of shares into the marketplace. Of course, new shares are always being issued, but these are locked up so that percentagewise there should not be much fundamental shift in the number of free trading shares, but volume-wise it will increase. More volume should, in theory, mean it is harder to shift the price higher or lower. Although this is countered by the fact that you would expect an Agglomeration™ to rise up quickly through the ranks of a $100m market cap to $500m and $1bn. At each of these milestones (and many intermediate ones), you will become accessible to bigger funds who decide to own you. And of course, bigger funds can buy bigger chunks of stock, negating the additional free float being added.

Is this a problem? Well, apart from the never-ending daily questions on the price, not really. For the investors we concentrate on, and the principals who own the most stock, they believe in the model and the focus on the fundamentals, not the daily variations. However, there are potentially a couple of ways that one could try and minimise the volatility. In a perfect world, you might have some 'friendly' institutional investors who believe in the model and basically say, for example, if the shares ever fall below ten times PE we will be a buyer, and if they ever go above twenty-five times PE we will be a seller. If they were big enough then this would in effect put a floor and a ceiling on the price – albeit there would still be a massive margin between those two ends of the equation, and they would need very deep pockets if the tide really turned. They would also have to be able to justify it internally which is never an easy thing to do when the tide is going against you. Imagine what those conversations would have sounded like as the Amazon share price rapidly tumbled down the side of a cliff? Or if you owned Apple stock that went sideways for two decades?

Despite the daily questions we receive as to why the share price has moved up, down or sideways, the reality is that we can't possibly know the individual motivations of investors and so, obviously, try and avoid getting sucked into conversations on the topic.

How Far Can This Go?

Business is as simple as changing the rules at the
beginning and then making the rules at the end.
— David and Tom Gardner, *The Motley
Fool's Rule Breakers, Rule Makers*[10]

I use that quote because when we did our first
Agglomeration™, David Kuo, CEO of Motley Fool
Asia, was interviewed about our model and while he
was broadly complimentary, he made the point that
companies coming in later, 'at the bottom' of the group,
as he put it, would not do as 'favourably' as those at
the top.[11]

---

10 David and Tom Gardner, *The Motley Fool's Rule Breakers, Rule Makers:
The Foolish Guide to Picking Stock* (Touchstone, 2010)
11 Channel News Asia, 'Strength in Unity – Collaborative IPO's, Agglomeration', YouTube (2016), www.youtube.com/watch?v=e1XgRwHxtwc

Mr Kuo may not have had much chance to research us before he was asked to make his comments, but his wording of 'top' and 'bottom' was suggestive of some kind of pyramid scheme, and I think this is worth addressing.

Absolutely, there is significantly more reward for those companies that join on day one, just as is the case for external investors. The value of their shares 'should' go up with each accretive acquisition that we do. However, there is also significantly more risk. We have many companies we talk to who love the model but would never commit to being involved before the company is listed, or even before it hits certain milestones (a year in the markets, a billion in market cap and so on). This is perfectly fine, and everyone has different risk appetites. So far, no different from any other IPO.

However, the inference of a pyramid suggests that for the model to work it needs to keep adding companies to the group. Yet that neglects to understand two key points. The first is that all the companies joining are typically debt free, profitable and cash-generating. The group could stop at three companies, thirty companies or 3,000. If all your companies are profitable and contributing then you can stop at any time, and indeed, at various points on the journey, the board might decide that an acquisition hiatus would be beneficial. However, the counter to that is that the board's role is the creation of long-term shareholder value for all shareholders. And if they are still able to buy ebit for less than it costs them to mint new shares, surely it would be against their fiduciary duties not to do so (assuming the opportunities to agglomerate good small businesses were still there)?

But the second point is equally important. Every company that joins the Agglomeration™ is asked to make a decision about doing so based on the share price remaining flat. Companies, like investors, are attracted to a share price that steadily climbs every week, but for obvious reasons that is not the primary reason we want companies to join. Remember, this model was originally designed to solve a problem for small businesses. The EPS accretive nature of the business is almost a happy (very happy) side effect of providing good small businesses with a scale advantage and liquidity in their stock. To that end, the ethos of an Agglomeration™ will always be to offer the services of the group to good businesses as long as it is done in a way that enhances value to existing shareholders.

Liquidity: Conclusion

Liquidity was the first of the three circles I looked at as an investor. Needless to say, it is fairly common among investors. Counterintuitively, there is actually a strong argument for an illiquidity premium. In the first instance, this relates to time horizons and in the second, it relates to human nature.

For time horizons it is recognised that investors, like Warren Buffett who can make decisions and be prepared to wait decades (or longer!) for the results, will likely gain significant returns. That premium comes even though once the decision is made to invest billions into large-scale infrastructure projects, these are not investments you can get in and out of if you should change your mind.

On the human nature front, there is a compelling argument to be made that some investment managers are choosing to tie their money up in untouchable decade-long PE funds for no other reason than to avoid the temptation to fiddle with allocations that might be more liquid. People are highly emotional and reactive to drawdowns in the market. If you don't feel you can stomach it, then removing the temptation to sell stock when everyone else is doing so might make perfect sense.

However, for me, as an investor, I favoured liquidity. Especially as, coming from an entrepreneurial background, I could see opportunities everywhere and the opportunity cost of having my money tied up for years or decades was just too painful. Sure, as I get older and wealthier, it is easier to move a portion of my investments into property or other asset classes that I might not be able to access for decades, but for my primary investment capital, liquidity is a must. A fast-growth, highly liquid stock on the capital markets certainly ticked that box.

Next, we will look at the second circle: *impact*.

IMPACT

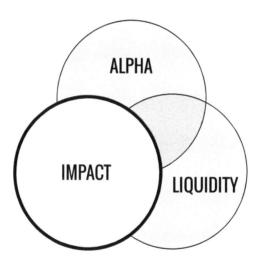

Impact investing aims to generate specific beneficial social or environmental effects in addition to financial gains.

A Trillion-Dollar Opportunity

According to research by J Ritter, Professor of Finance at the University of Florida, if you held shares in a company and sold it at the end of their first day's public listing, on average, your return would be 17.9%.[12] If you held for a year, your return would be 23.4%.

How do you consistently get access to pre-IPO shares?

The second of the three circles is *impact*. 'Impact investing' means different things to different people

12 Jay R Ritter, 'Initial Public Offerings: Updated Statistics on Long-run Performance' (2019), https://site.warrington.ufl.edu/ritter/files/2019/04/IPOs2018_Longrun-Returns.pdf

and I'm probably not helping the cause by co-opting it for my own needs, but for me impact was specifically being able to see the impact of my investment. As my wealth increased, more and more of the investment opportunities I was being presented with promised to be very rewarding financially, but it was getting less and less clear what exactly it was I was investing in. While my investment manager was keen I should invest in his products, he couldn't really articulate what exactly it was he wanted me to buy, or more specifically, he couldn't explain what was happening to my money when I purchased these clever, structured note products, hedged against currencies, downturns, upturns and U-turns.

I realised what I liked was investing my money into a company and seeing the impact of that money in the form of new jobs being created or new products being developed. Call me old-fashioned, but I wanted to know my money was doing something useful.

So, if I wanted to invest directly into a business, what were my options? Did that mean I should become an angel investor?

No angel

A few years ago, I received a message on LinkedIn from Baybars Altuntas, the president of the World

Business Angel Investment Forum (WBAF), he had read our book and loved what we were doing.

After a bit of digging, I discovered that Baybars was actually an incredible entrepreneur (and a fixture on the Turkish version of *Dragons Den* or *Shark Tank*) and he was now focused on building a global network of angel investors to support the start-up ecosystem around the world. Although Agglomeration™ is most definitely not aimed at start-up or early-stage businesses, what Baybars had identified was that many of the angels in his network ended up with dozens of holdings in small businesses that would never become the unicorns they had once dreamt of but were developing into decent businesses in their own right. Agglomeration™ offered a great opportunity for these businesses to grow and for the angels to get some liquidity back.

To cut a long story short, he ended up offering me the position of high commissioner to Singapore for the WBAF. Well – I'm a sucker for a good job title and you have to admit it was a good one!

The problem was I had always been sceptical about angel investing. Firstly, after years of being an entrepreneur going out trying to raise capital, I was about the worst person start-ups should come to with their pitches about how, even though they had achieved nothing to date, if they could just 'capture 1% of the market' we would all be billionaires. As a wise man once said, 'You can't bullshit a bullshitter' and I would struggle to bite my tongue when I saw these pitches.

Secondly, there was another aspect to angel investing that was starting to raise red flags for me. As the cost of the capital needed to 'build out' technology, or roll out technology solutions, had dropped away, so the funds necessary to become an angel had dropped significantly. Now, for as little as $10–20k you could invest in a company. A whole bunch of very bored corporate middle managers were starting to flood into angel investing. I understood the appeal. If you are a middle manager at some giant corporate, you have a whole bunch of millennial employees who don't listen to you, and a bunch of senior managers who don't care about you, and you and your peers are just fighting it out for the chance to win ever-diminishing 'better' job titles and more responsibility.

For $10k not only do you now have something interesting to talk about at dinner parties, but you have a bunch of poor entrepreneurs who are duty bound to hang off your every word, even though you have zero experience of running a start-up.

Lowering the barriers to entry meant there were many more angels in the marketplace, but I wasn't sure that was necessarily a good thing for genuine entrepreneurs.

However, despite my jaded nature and natural cynicism, the title of 'high commissioner' was too good to resist and I found myself making an annual pilgrimage to Istanbul to meet with angels from around the world. What I found among the many truly excellent people I met there was that I was missing a bigger picture. Or rather I was viewing it through the lens of an investor and actually almost every angel I met there had a very different view of the world. Where I looked at a start-up and thought there is a one in a million opportunity that I would ever see my money again, true angels looked at that start-up and thought (rightly or wrongly), 'I can help this company slash its odds of failure through my knowledge and contacts. And maybe, just maybe, we can together get a fantastic exit in the future. But even if we don't it will be a fun ride and I will learn a lot along the way.'

The angels I spoke to there were all very aware that this was unlikely to be a very profitable endeavour, but it was one that they found deeply rewarding in other areas and that I found to be admirable. The problem really lay in the term angel 'investor' – this was much more akin to gambling or probably more like having a very expensive hobby that brings you a lot of joy. A bit like collecting wine as an 'investment' because you enjoy the process of finding, selecting and curating the wines and now you can justify it as an investment. But then drinking it. It's definitely rewarding, but not as useful as other investments for putting the kids through college!

Even the 'top' angels who were wheeled out on stage for their amazing ability to spot gold in the rough would freely admit in private that often their losses far outweighed their gains and had they kept their money in the bank it would have made better returns. But it was something they seemed to enjoy immensely.

As glad as I was that these people exist and are willing to pour their time and money into these fledgling businesses, it was clear that a hobby of angel investing was not for me. As the Dragons say, 'For that reason, I'm out!'

(If you do like that space and fancy polishing your halo, I recommend getting along to the annual WBAF event – there are some truly wonderful people from around the world. Have a look at: www.wbaforum.org)

Not angels but spinning wheels

So, if angel investing wasn't my thing, what was? I realised that I liked businesses that had successfully got through that awkward start-up phase and were well established. And once again it came down to impact. You give $1m to a start-up, they are as likely to spend that money on social media marketing as anything else while they try and buy market share. If they haven't figured out their product market fit yet, they will still be stuck spinning their wheels, it's just your money has allowed them to spin their wheels much faster.

However, you give that $1m to a successful, but very unglamorous, air-conditioning maintenance company that has been in business for twenty years and they know exactly what levers to pull to turn that $1m into $2m or more. In most cases, a successful small business like that has been turning down clients because they didn't have the resources to expand. They know exactly what to do with your money to get the best results.

I realised one big difference between early-stage and established businesses. When you talk to an early-stage business all they talk about is the future and it's always rosy. When you talk to an established business, they are able to talk about what they have already achieved. Plus, they normally have some amazing war stories – and to me it is in the war stories that we learn the lessons that allow us to grow.

That SMEs make up more than 50% of the global economy in developed countries does not seem to be open to dispute.[13] That the entire finance world hasn't figured out how to profit from them directly also seems not to be in dispute. In fact, as a rule of thumb, a business would have to reach at least $100m in revenue just to get on the radar of the finance industry. (Since the cost of typical due diligence is basically the same whether you are a $10m or a $100m company, PE typically doesn't see enough margins to justify the expense of going below $100m.)

It's not that the finance world doesn't want to, it is simply that your average small business is just too illiquid and too risky for sophisticated capital to risk getting involved.

Start-ups, unicorns and other nonsense

We've already touched on angels and start-ups and why they're not for me, but you cannot deny the impact that Silicon Valley has had on the global collective mind when it comes to business investing.

This 'Silicon Valley model' quickly spread around the world. You would be hard pressed to find a government anywhere that hasn't at least paid lip service

---

13 Christopher Arnold, 'The Foundation for Economies Worldwide Is Small Business', *IFAC* (2019), www.ifac.org/knowledge-gateway/ practice-management/discussion/foundation-economies-world-wide-small-business

to being the next Silicon Valley. The money poured into the ecosystem and suddenly anyone with a hair-brained idea could quit their job, buy a quirky domain with no vowels in it and call themselves an entrepreneur.

Meanwhile, the traditional small business community looked on in wonder. The twenty-year-old business with staff, customers, profit and cash that was wholly unappealing to the investor realised that, in this new paradigm, old-fashioned metrics like profits or cash-flow were kryptonite to investors. What you needed was a flashy deck and a graph showing a hockey stick pointing to the moon. The hockey stick need not be revenue or profit either, it could be eyeballs or down-loads or clicks or users or basically anything that could grow exponentially. Whether you could deliver or not was almost secondary to whether you could raise the next round of funds.

Now don't get me wrong, all business is a game and the Silicon Valley game is a very good one if you know how to play it. Plus, there are countless great businesses out there today that would never have been able to grow organically and have relied on the belief and support of early investors to allow them to over-come the many obstacles of starting a small business.

Also, as a consumer, I'm particularly grateful to VCs subsidising my experiences as some of these start-ups offer incredible services for next to nothing as they rush to land new customers.

And yet, for all the media attention, the government grants, the corporate sponsorship, the endless pitch fests, incubators, hackathons and so on, *ad nauseam*, most money flowed to those who were trying to figure out how to start and run businesses. *Not* to those who had already figured this out. With all that money flowing around, not one cent of it was going to traditional businesses. Plumbing companies rarely do hockey stick returns (although they are good for liquidity – boom boom!).

Entrepreneurs are resourceful, they don't get this far in life without being so. Some find a way to cobble a solution together, some take on a personal guarantee and occasionally the stress of it destroys them. And most just play it safe. Like me in my office fifteen years ago – I'd phone up the client, apologise and turn down the biggest contract, the contract that could have doubled the size of my business. Meanwhile, in Omaha, Warren Buffett keeps reading the papers, hoping to find a home for his $100m that week which will deliver better returns than an index tracker.

What was becoming clear was outside of the world of start-ups and angels and Silicon Valley and VCs there was a real world of opportunity that was apparently being completely overlooked.

A finance revolution?

Michael Milken is an interesting Wall Street character. 'Wiser' readers will remember him from his 'junk bond' days in the 1980s. Younger readers may know of him from his philanthropic efforts and the Milken Institute event on the West Coast of America that is trying to rival the World Economic Forum in Davos, Switzerland.

Although I had heard his name, it was his starring role in *Den of Thieves*, one of the all-time classic books about eighties' business by James B Stewart,[14] that really brought his innovation home to me. If you're not familiar with the story, Michael Milken is credited with the invention, or at the very least the greatest exploitation, of the concept of 'junk bonds' – today more commonly known as 'high-yield bonds'. What he worked out, before anyone else, was that these junk bonds paid much higher returns than the premium bonds but didn't actually tend to default nearly as often as you would think. Hence, you were getting high-risk returns, without as much high risk as you might expect. *Institutional Investor* called this the 'greatest invention in the recent history of finance'.[15]

---

14 James B Stewart, *Den of Thieves* (Simon & Schuster Ltd, 1992)
15 William D Cohan, 'The Michael Milken Project: How did a 70-year-old ex-con barred for life from Wall Street become one of its most respected men?', *Institutional Investor* (2017), www.institutionalinvestor.com/article/b1f6wj9ghqxv8h/The-Michael-Milken-Project

What it did was give corporations with limited credit ratings and consequently low access to capital access to a new source of funding. Entire industries suddenly flourished, businesses boomed, jobs were created, wealth snowballed.

Today in small business there has been no such revolution. But what if there was a similar invention that could suddenly unlock capital for the small business world?

The Birth of the Accelerated Venture Capital (AVC) Fund

For all we believed that Agglomeration™ had the potential to be one of the most significant financial innovations for small business, there was one hole in the model which soon became apparent.

For the quick thinking among you, you will have realised that while Agglomeration™ solved many problems for small business, there was nothing in the model that was about injecting capital *into* the business. It was not designed for that; it was designed to solve the problem of scale and liquidity. Yes, they could now go after bigger deals as a PLC, but would they actually have the resources to serve the client?

A good friend of mine, Sarah, owned a small media company in Asia. It was niche and successful and, for all the talk of the publishing industry dying, it had some great corporate clients who paid good money to produce beautiful in-house magazines. The business was well established, my friend was highly regarded, and the company margins were good. Each year the business made about $5m in revenue and profits hovered around the $1m mark. It was a publishing industry, so the constant need to hit deadlines aside, it was a good example of a relatively stress-free 'lifestyle' business. She liked her team; she liked her clients; and she enjoyed the commensurate perks.

But then an opportunity came along. One of her favourite and longstanding clients asked her if she would be interested in a new project. They only wanted to work with her and were willing to pay a premium to do so. This one project would nearly double the size of her business in one fell swoop. And it was guaranteed for five years. In short, it was the sort of perfect contract that entrepreneurs dream about. But this was no fluke, it was a result of twenty years of hard-earned respect in her industry and ten years of having built up a professional and profitable media business, focused on its clients, and now perfectly placed to benefit from this opportunity.

Except ... She would need about $3m of capital to build the capacity and hire the right team in order to make the project work. Up until that point, she had not taken on any outside investors. Although she had occasionally had to borrow the odd $10k or $20k from her friends and family to cover payroll in the early days, she was proud of the way she had bootstrapped things and was glad she didn't have an investor to answer to. But this opportunity was too big and too exciting to turn down. She decided to go out and raise some capital.

Six months later and the woman in front of me in a busy Hong Kong coffee shop was a shadow of her former self. Nearly in tears she told me a story I had heard countless times from many business owners. Despite the great business she was sitting on and the fantastic opportunity she had in front of her, she had been unable to raise a single dollar. She had gone from being widely respected in her industry to being a newbie in the fundraising game and she hated it. Most of the time she couldn't even get a meeting with those companies who would supposedly be a good starting point. When she did, she never got to meet anyone senior, it was normally some intern who had been taught the phrase 'What's your USP?' (unique selling point) and didn't understand why anyone would read a magazine if they had a phone.

She lowered her sights and started talking to individual investors. Only to discover that most of them used the term 'investor' to get interesting meetings, but when push came to shove, they often seemed to have less money than she did.

The reality was, for her, and for most small businesses, that going out and trying to get access to capital is a soul-destroying activity that is time intensive and rarely yields anything close to the results you want.

As we drank our coffees, we discussed Agglomeration™. While it would certainly be a good option for her at some point in the future, it didn't solve her immediate need for capital to grow. I put her in touch with some real investors I knew might be interested, and promised to think about whether there was a better way we could help her.

Ticking all the circles

That meeting had come at an interesting time for me, because as well as the Agglomeration™ work I was doing, I was also starting to think more about my own investment decisions and criteria. Like the three circles on the front of this book, I had realised that I wanted my investments to tick all three boxes. As big a believer as I was in Agglomeration™ – in fact I had backed it with almost everything I had – I was conscious that when I was buying shares on the open market, I wasn't directly helping the individual companies, I was merely putting money into the pockets of earlier investors.

Now of course there was a secondary benefit that every company that joined would get. Being part of a PLC, they should now be able to win much bigger contracts and that should, in theory, lead to job creation which, as discussed, was the kind of impact I wanted to be having. And obviously, the more buyers of the stock, the higher the value of that stock would go. Yet, it was still a secondary benefit, not a primary benefit. A primary benefit would be if I, as an investor, took the money out of my bank and gave it to the entrepreneur for them to deploy as they best saw fit. That would ideally be resourcing up in order to secure some new contract.

Like my own business needs many years before, my friend's need for capital would tick my impact investing criteria. It would help a great small business to resource up in order to solve a client's problem and would make a significant impact on the profits of that business. What it could not definitely do is tick the other two boxes for me. It would not provide me with liquidity, and it was pretty hard to judge whether it would offer me significant alpha.

Ultimately, that would depend on whether I could then sell my stake in her business in the future at a higher price than I had come in for. The multiples you get for a $1m profit company are not vastly improved when you jump to a $2m profit company.

Similar to the angel investors we explored earlier, the intention would have been good, the results would no doubt have been excellent for the entrepreneur and the impact would probably have been another five to ten jobs created, but could I honestly believe that this was a good investment for me?

As I walked away from the meeting there was a third issue that had been tickling me for a while without a good resolution. Not every company was looking for capital when it joined an Agglomeration™, but when companies in the group started winning bigger contracts then, without fail, they were going to need that capital to scale up. We had talked about perhaps raising money at the holding company level and offering out soft loans to companies, but wouldn't it be better if they had their own capital in the first place?

What we needed was an investor with deep pockets who shared our view of the world and would be willing to write a cheque to these small businesses just before they joined an Agglomeration™.

I got back to my hotel and started drawing all over the branded letter paper on the desk (pausing long enough to wonder if people actually still wrote letters). Basically, we needed to find a fund that would be able to go out and raise capital and then invest in our small businesses, just before they got acquired. We, as the PLC, would then not only be acquiring profitable businesses, those businesses would also already be cashed up and ready to exploit the advantages of going public. That would mean that for every acquisition the PLC did, it could announce to the market that it had just acquired, for example, $1m of earnings before interest, tax, depreciation and amortisation (ebitda).

Ebitda and $3m of net cash. And we were still paying less than five times ebitda plus what was on the balance sheet for it, making it value-enhancing for existing shareholders.

A virtuous circle

The first person I cold called with the concept wrote me a cheque for a $100m on the spot and we all lived happily ever after.

Of course, it didn't happen like that! Either through my lack of ability to articulate it well or an industry-wide resistance to anything new (or more likely a combination of both), I found myself in the same shoes as my publishing friend: I was trying to pitch to funds that had zero interest in listening to me. After dozens of these meetings I had my first breakthrough.

Back in Singapore, I phoned up a fund manager whom I had met several years before and asked him if he would be open to a coffee and me bouncing a new fund idea off him. This gentleman had been in the fund business longer than I had been alive and kindly agreed to drop by our office and hear me out.

I took him into our boardroom and started enthusiastically explaining the model and drawing out on our wall how the flow of money would work. Stoically, he watched my efforts, occasionally nodded and took a few notes. At the end of my presentation, I said, 'So what do you think? As far as I can tell nobody has ever done anything like this before.'

'That's not true,' he replied, 'we've been doing this exact same thing for twenty-plus years. In fact, one of our funds is specifically designed to invest into the same space as yours: companies doing $1–5m in ebitda.'

Somewhat surprisingly, I found myself to be more excited that it wasn't a new idea than I was disappointed that I wasn't as clever as I thought I was. At least, I reasoned to myself, if they have been doing this for twenty years, they will see the value in it and might be our first investor.

He went on.

'There is one small difference with our model that yours has solved. Just like you, we invest the cash into these small businesses. But in your model, you immediately take them public. In our model, we sit and pray for five years that we can find an exit for them. I like your model much more, you will make more money in one year than all our funds can make in their lifetime.' And he burst out laughing.

Finally, the breakthrough we were looking for!

'Fantastic,' I said, 'would you be interested in partnering with us and being the fund that invests?'

'No, no, no. Sadly our fund only invests in South East Asia companies. Your business is global and that wouldn't work for us, but I'm sure you'll be very successful.' And with that he finished his coffee and headed off.

The problem wasn't unique to him. As my quick introduction to the world of funds revealed, they can only invest in what they have raised capital to invest in. Which I guess makes sense, and yet it left me with what seemed like the perfect virtuous circle of wealth creation but with one vital missing component. Even when we could find open-ended funds that had the discretion to invest, they were very clear that they would only invest when we had a two- to three-year-track record.

If you can't beat 'em, join 'em

What I really didn't want to do was to have to start my own fund, but if we were unable to get anyone else to partner with us, that was increasingly looking like the only option. Apart from the complexity and financial regulations, we would then have to be the ones who went out and raised capital for the fund, when we were also trying to encourage investors in our PLC. One new thing at a time was already more than enough for most investors.

But if no one else was going to partner with us, it did become our only option, and after months of searching we found a great partner who would manage our fund. We just had to provide the investment criteria and the funds themselves.

As I continued to take the model around and pitch it to various potential funds to partner with, my empathy grew for my friend Sarah and the other business owners like her who try and raise capital. I am quite sure it is significantly easier to do this today than it was twenty years ago, but it is still a pretty soul-destroying experience.

Obviously, from our perspective the bigger the ticket size (funds we raise in one go) the more we could achieve, but when you get to the funds that can potentially write big cheques you tend to be dealing with employees – and for them the equation is very simple. A meeting with a new entrepreneurial idea is more interesting than working at their desk and so they will take them all day. But a new entrepreneurial idea carries career risk. There is little to no upside for an employee taking a risk on a new fund. But there is plenty of downside if it goes wrong. Hence, despite many promising conversations, no one was willing to invest in our first year. We lowered our sights and went back to our investor base that already knew, liked and trusted us, and that allowed us to get our first investments. With this approach we were finally able to start raising some capital into the AVC Fund.

The idea in a nutshell

The model was very simple. Big institutions would fund AVC. AVC would invest those funds exclusively into small businesses that had already agreed to join an Agglomeration™. Basically, in a back-to-back transaction, AVC would invest in the business and the business would be acquired by the PLC.

In the diagram below, let's assume that our small business has $1m of ebit, AVC invests $3m into the business in the morning and later that day the small business gets acquired by the PLC for five times ebit plus whatever is on the balance sheet (the difference between the three times the business owner gets and the five times the PLC is paid is made up of introducers' fees, taxes, legal fees, Unity Group costs and so on).

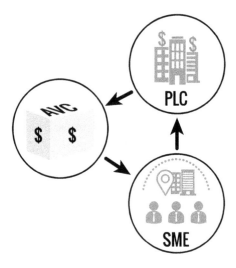

AVC would invest in the business and the business would be acquired by the PLC

For the small business, this was off the charts great. Not only would they get to go public for no cost using the Agglomeration™ model, they would also have a war chest with which they could utilise their new-found status to scale up. The more they grew, the more profit they earned, the more stock they would accumulate through the perpetual earn-in model. Who could turn that down? To be absolutely clear, this is not a loan, this is an equity investment. AVC buys stock in the company, there is no need for the company to pay anyone back. What's more, it is an equity investment without a needy investor with different time horizons from the business owner.

For the PLC that was acquiring the business there was an immediate benefit. In effect the PLC could announce to the marketplace they had just acquired $1m of ebit and $3m of net cash and had paid a total of $8m in shares ($5m for ebit plus the $3m on the balance sheet). You would be hard pressed to find other PLCs that could acquire cash and ebit so cheaply. However, more importantly the companies that came into the group now had a much higher chance of success and, from a risk mitigation point of view, a significantly reduced risk of one of the companies failing. In fact, a small business that was debt free, profitable and sitting on a healthy cash balance would need to work pretty hard to go bust in its first few years in the group. The combination of these factors makes each acquisition extremely value-enhancing to the existing shareholders. There was also a secondary benefit for the PLC which I'll touch on when we discuss terms.

What about AVC? AVC had, in effect, just invested $3m into a small private company and almost immediately that company had got its exit. Unlike the founders of the company, AVC's shares were not locked up, meaning that as soon as the share price rose, they would be able to start exiting their position at a premium. That ability to exit quickly is the key, because for every dollar they are able to pull out of their investment, they are able to invest that dollar in the next small business, meaning that there is a compounding effect to the earnings that are made.

Basically, it is like offering someone the chance to invest in twenty-plus companies a year that are debt-free, profitable and about to go public. Who wouldn't take that opportunity?

The terms of the deal

Small business owners who want to join an Agglomeration™ and get access to the AVC funds need to submit a business plan to the AVC Fund managers and the Fund has absolute discretion on whether or not they will invest. In fact, they do due diligence on each company coming into an Agglomeration™ in parallel.

It is not quite as simple as us giving a suitcase of cash to the business owner on day one. Firstly, while the money has been allocated to the small business, they do not actually get access to any of the funds until they have been in the PLC and have been a 'good corporate citizen' for six months – that is, submitted their financials on time, played nicely with the other kids in the group and so on.

Secondly, the business plan needs to request the funds in tranches with key deliverables to be hit before the next tranche is released. For example, if the Fund has invested $3m, the business owner might draw down the first million and have to hit certain targets they themselves set and agree before they get access to the rest of the funds.

As touched on above, this has a secondary very positive impact on the PLC. With every AVC-sponsored acquisition, the PLC balance sheet looks healthier and healthier. In fact, it is possible that some or all of that money may be retained at the holding company level indefinitely until such time as the subsidiary has met its obligations and hit its targets. And of course, not every subsidiary will hit its targets so the money will stay with the PLC.

(For those wondering about the actual mechanics of the money flow, AVC does not actually invest the cash directly in the business, but in a special-purpose vehicle called an SPV, which we create to acquire the business. This SPV typically also holds Unity Group's shares, any introducer shares, and so on. The SPV including AVC's capital and the assets of the business are then acquired by the PLC.)

What's in it for the institutions?

So why would an institution invest in AVC rather than just into the PLC?

Firstly, during the first few years of an Agglomeration™, the bigger institutions wouldn't be able to invest directly. Imagine an institution whose minimum ticket size was $100m trying to buy shares in a company that has only a $100m market cap. It wouldn't work. However, it could invest that $100m in AVC, which could convert that into twenty lots of $5m to provide growth capital for small businesses joining the group and so the institution gets to benefit from the growth story.

Additionally, AVC offers two especially unique advantages over competitors in the marketplace. Typically, that would be either PE or traditional VC. Most of the PE deals currently floating around are what's known as 8+1+1: basically, your money is locked up for between eight and ten years. In VC it is even worse. Increasingly, VC outfits are unable to return money to their partners for nearer to fourteen years because there are so few exits available.[16]

---

16 Diane Mulcahy, 'The New Reality of the 14-Year Venture Capital Fund', *Institutional Investor* (2015), www.institutionalinvestor.com/article/b14z9vv7hjbt6y/the-new-reality-of-the-14-year-venture-capital-fund

Although there are some positives associated with a lack of liquidity, for most investors the opportunity cost of being locked up for that long far outweighs the potential benefits. However, with little other choice, huge amounts of money continue to be pumped into these two sectors. By contrast, because AVC can get liquid almost immediately, we can offer our investors a twelve-month lock-up rather than a twelve-year one.

There is a reason we called our fund *Accelerated Venture Capital*!

The second benefit AVC can offer is transparency. When you invest funds into a PE or VC fund, you will typically get a quarterly report of how your funds are doing, but more often than not it is the fund itself that is valuing its own investments. A well-known VC approach is to make a large investment at a low valuation of a start-up and then, six to twelve months later, make a small investment at a much higher valuation. Since valuation is based on the last shares traded, the value of the initial investment is now seen to have grown substantially. At least that is what they can tell their investors.

With AVC there is no such opportunity to fudge the numbers – the model is deliberately fully transparent. The institution invests in AVC, AVC invests a portion of that into an SME, the SME reverses into the PLC and AVC starts to sell down its position as soon as it can do so in a positive way. At all points during the twelve months, AVC can be completely open with the investors about where the money is in the cycle and exactly how much return it has made so far. Transparency tends to mean no nasty shocks at the end of the investment term.

Conflicts of interest?

One question that does come up concerns a conflict of interest with the PLC. The Fund, being independent, has to work in the best interests of its investors, not necessarily in the best interests of the PLC. Obviously, in an ideal world, the PLC wouldn't want AVC to sell any shares as that could conceivably limit the growth, or even create downward momentum in the stock. While that's true, AVC does have pretty aligned interests with the PLC, given that at any time it is likely to be holding stock from multiple deals and have multiple deals still coming through.

For the PLC, as with volatility being the price of above-market returns, AVC selling down is the price of getting significant volumes of growth capital into the businesses in the group. Most PLCs I know would happily take that deal.

The AVC Fund was created and received its first funding in late 2018. It has already made its first investment and at the time of writing was targeting its first exit for 50% return within twelve months. Our ambition for it is simple: the more funds we can get into it, the greater the number of small businesses we can capitalise and the more AVC can compound its gains.

With Agglomeration™ providing the platform for liquidity, AVC could potentially inject significant growth capital into a segment of the business world that has been long overlooked.

Too good to be true?

No product is perfect and even more so than the underlying Agglomeration™, AVC is susceptible to a hit on the share price. If the shares of the PLC were to go below the strike price that AVC came in at, then it would only really have twelve months to hope the price recovers. A year might seem like a long time, but it does have a habit of flying by.

There are two key tools we have in our toolbox to try and solve that risk. The first is that it is within the mandate of AVC to use funds to buy Agglomeration™ stock on the open market if it feels that it is undervalued. It basically plays the role of a benevolent institutional buyer. Secondly, the board of any Agglomeration™ PLC also has a mandate to use its capital to buy shares if it feels they are undervalued. Just like the Teledyne case study in Section One, if there are too many sellers in the market the Agglomeration™ will buy its own shares back. The effect of this combined buy side, the buyers in the market, should hopefully create a floor in the market, preventing trade below a certain price.

The world is changing

It has long been accepted that the role of a corporation is the creation of shareholder value. At least it has long been accepted in the USA, the biggest market that has an impact globally. Corporate CEOs agreed with this concept of existing for the shareholders' benefit and Wall Street certainly agreed, rewarding with glee any efforts to cut costs and increase profits.

Yet once again there seemed to be a big disconnect between finance and the business world. What I was seeing in business was it was getting increasingly hard to find entrepreneurs, staff or customers who thought the sole responsibility of a business was to increase shareholder value. In fact, it was becoming clear that if your business didn't stand for something beyond just making money you were going to have a hard time attracting the best and the brightest to either work with you or spend money with you. And yet this seemed to appal investors.

I remember trying to understand this line of thinking as I sat with a financial adviser. His view was very clear that the company should maximise profits 'at all costs' and then he and his clients should be free to use that money in whatever way they chose, supporting whatever cause was important to them, not what cause was important to whoever the current CEO of the company was.

It just seemed perverse to me. While I understood the logic, it didn't gel with what I was seeing in the business community or the consumer world, and it seemed to be a short-sighted approach.

The extension of this idea I found even harder to stomach, despite being very atypical of many of the investors I have met. The adviser's view was that not only should the CEOs of companies not be concerning themselves with moral/ethical issues just to appease staff and customers, but that investors themselves should stop trying to pick and choose investments based on ethics. He found the whole idea of ESG (ethics, social and governance) funds to be a blatant fraud designed purely to make people feel virtuous and smug. He strongly recommended his clients should invest in companies that I would typically steer clear of such as tobacco or the arms industry. His argument was that he would rather his clients profited from these great businesses than someone with less ethics and that once his clients had made their profits, they were once again free to give them to whichever worthy causes they liked.

I envied this black and white approach to the world but while I could understand his point of view, it again showed me how disconnected 'typical' finance was from the small business world I knew. Every investor is an 'activist' in the sense that owning stock shows your support for that business. Selling your stock, or not owning it in the first place, is a great way to show your displeasure with products or ethics and, ultimately, business being business, if there is not enough market, they will either innovate their way out of it or the business will wither and die.

While you can't control who buys your stock on the open market, through meeting enough investors I was able to find those who seemed to have more of a value match with us. Typically, they tended to be entrepreneurial, often coming from a small business background and so sharing an empathy and an understanding for small business challenges.

Quite early on I accidentally discovered a quick litmus test of where people stood. I called it the 'Elon Musk Test'.

ELON MUSK

Is Elon Musk swimming naked?

Whether you agree with Elon Musk's approach to business or not is probably a good indication of whether you're an entrepreneur or a professional investor.

There are numerous ways in which investors and entrepreneurs differ in their views and values but, in my research, I have been staggered by how polarising Musk is.

Of course, if you're an entrepreneur, it is likely that all you see in your feed is stories about what an amazing real-life Tony Stark he is. As a consumer, maybe you admire the products he makes and as a citizen, perhaps you think anything that reduces pollution in cities is a good thing? Reading outside your 'bubble' is always a cultural shock but it is necessary if you want to understand exactly what Wall Street has against him.

At the heart of it seems to be a deep-seated mistrust of self-promotion and over-promising. Often the very things that allow entrepreneurs to attract clients, staff and investors to grow the business are not what investors want to see when it goes public and 'should' have a level of maturity. It is the time to bring in the 'grown-ups'. But grown-ups are, by their nature, risk averse and to push beyond the norm you need someone who is willing to stake it all on the line.

In Silicon Valley, the model of move fast and break things, try and solve big global problems (moonshots) and use scale to solve almost any problem is not just lore, it is almost hard-wired into the thinking of entrepreneurs from the Valley (and increasingly from the rest of the world). That model, no doubt, has many problems but it has also been responsible for some amazing developments over the years.

But it doesn't always work. Elizabeth Holmes, of Theranos fame, built a $9bn house of cards on false promises in the hope that the technology would catch up with the narrative she was sharing.

Holmes was caught because the technology didn't catch up. Not even close. And a determined journalist was able to unravel the true story. Unlike Theranos, most such cases don't unravel when times are good, they fall apart when times are bad, when no more money can be raised to plug the gaps. The argument on Wall Street is that Musk's self-promotion (flamethrowers, rocket launches, caps, tunnel digging, kid-rescuing subs, twitter pronouncements, etc) is nothing more than a distraction and that when the money runs out, Tesla will fall off a cliff and the hand-wringing will begin. As of October 2018, there were increasingly loud voices on the Street saying the party was about to end. And as Warren Buffett says, 'Only when the tide goes out do you discover who has been swimming naked.'

Will that be Musk? Or will he get Tesla to profitability, justify the lofty share price and have the last laugh on Wall Street? Will it even matter? Entrepreneurs will possibly still admire his resolve and investors will possibly never trust him. How you feel on the matter probably says a lot about where you sit on that spectrum.[17]

---

17 Callum Laing, 'Elon Musk', *The Asian Entrepreneur* (2018), www.asianentrepreneur.org/elon-musk. This is based on an abridged version of Callum Laing's article, 'Elon Musk'. Original article available at the link above.

Part of the perceived problem with Musk is that he views his companies as vehicles to drive global change in behaviour. But that definitely doesn't gel with the idea of companies existing to increase shareholder value. Yet as I said earlier, the world is changing. In August 2019, the Business Round Table, comprising 200 of the USA's top CEOs, decided that the view of corporations was too narrow and shareholder value was no longer their main incentive: '… investing in employees, delivering value to customers, dealing ethically with suppliers and supporting outside communities are now at the forefront of American business goals'.[18]

This seemed much more in line with what I was seeing, but then again, the real proof is in the pudding. Will the corporations match the words with the heart and, more importantly, will it matter to Wall Street or will they be punished for this 'profit second' approach?

---

18 Maggie Fitzgerald, 'The CEOs of nearly 200 companies just said shareholder value is no longer their main objective', CNBC (2019), www.cnbc.com/amp/2019/08/19/the-ceos-of-nearly-two-hundred-companies-say-shareholder-value-is-no-longer-their-main-objective.html

Impact: Conclusion

A t the end of the day, it was apparent that people had some pretty strong feelings on this topic. A little like the old adage of 'never talk politics or religion', I knew I was unlikely to change anyone's mind and yet I could control what I invested in. All other things being equal, I wanted to invest in good businesses where my money could make a real difference in terms of allowing the company to grow, to hire people and to deliver more value.

The problem was that all other things were not equal. Until we came up with AVC Fund there was no way to invest directly into a small business and have liquidity. By combining AVC with the Agglomeration™

model, a new financial product now existed that could not only inject capital into the businesses, but do so just before they went public, providing the valuable liquidity. This was potentially the product that Warren Buffett could invest in that could offer incredible growth.

We have never had problems attracting small businesses who want to join an Agglomeration™. But just imagine that we go out to market with a fully funded AVC Fund behind us. Our pitch to small businesses basically becomes: 'At no cost to yourselves, we will take you public AND we will invest up to three times your ebitda to allow you to grow.'

Until this book, we have not really gone public with the AVC model. Even without it, we are getting 1,000 applications a year from small businesses wanting to join Agglomerations™. Can you imagine the stampede when business owners realise they can take their company public and get funding? Can you imagine what happens to the value of the shares of any holding company that enables accretive profit to businesses that happen to be sitting on their own growth capital?

AVC/Agglomeration™ might not be the junk bonds moment that corporations had thirty-plus years ago, but it most definitely feels as if there is demand from the investment world to not miss out on half of the economy and there is no question that there is demand from small business to use capital to grow. Whether it is us, or whether it is some other innovation, at some point there has to be a way to reconnect the capital with the people who create the value! There are a lot of jobs and livelihoods relying on it.

In the final section you will see how we combine the two elements and get to our third circle – alpha.

SECTION THREE

ALPHA

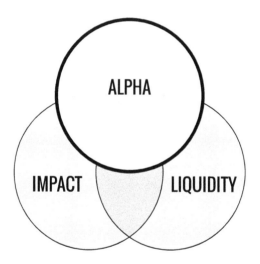

'**Alpha**' (the Greek letter α) is a term used in investing to describe a strategy's ability to beat the market, or its 'edge'. Alpha is thus also often referred to as 'excess return'.

— James Chen, *Investopedia*[19]

19 James Chen, 'Alpha', *Investopedia* (2019), www.investopedia.com/ terms/a/alpha.asp

The 'Holy Grail' Of Investing

In Section One, 'Liquidity', we saw how Agglomeration™ is a game-changer for small business. For the first time ever, it unlocks the value in small business by turning it into a highly liquid, high-yielding and fast-scaling financial product for the investment community.

In Section Two, we saw that a unique fund structure, AVC, changes the small business funding environment forever. Allowing big institutions to invest hundreds of millions and split it into scores, or hundreds, of small businesses, transforming their ability to scale, yet in a product framework that allows the institutions to exit after twelve months, if they so desire.

In this final section, we put it all together and present a case study of Multiple Business Holdings (MBH) Corporation PLC, a current example of how this can work now and in the future, and what it means to you the investor. We finish up by peering into the future. A long way into the future.

It's all a game

In 2017, I started running a one-and-a-half-day Agglomeration™ workshop in Singapore a couple of times a year. Ostensibly, this was for the incoming business owners. With companies wanting to join us from all around the world, often we would get 90% through the process of acquiring them without ever actually having met them face to face (the due diligence team might have been on site, but let's be honest, due diligence guys are not generally renowned for their relationship-building skills!). During this workshop, we could get to know owners a bit better, they could get to know us in person, and we could talk through any concerns they might have.

Over time the workshop evolved, and a few things became apparent: this wasn't just a 'nice to have', this was a really important aspect in making sure expectations were aligned on both sides and that we had companies joining that truly understood what this was all about. It was also an essential tool to train them on some of the fundamental differences between being a small private company and what was about to change when they became part of a big PLC.

However, we also started to have investors coming to us and asking if they could attend. Finally, we had partners and introducers (the network of individuals who often refer us to these companies) who in some cases were out there over-selling the concept which then caused us problems trying to trim back the expectations of business owners.

To meet demand, the frequency of these events increased, but the results that we were getting weren't really delivering. Maybe because investors, introducers and business owners have very different needs from and expectations of such an event, it was difficult to tailor it to each group. The workshop evolved into a basic 'dump' of all the content, strategies and tactics, and each individual had to pick and choose what was relevant to them.

This was not satisfactory. I noticed that people were leaving these sessions focused on a few tactics that seemed important to them, but not really grasping the underlying fundamentals that had driven the selection of those tactics. Additionally, from a purely selfish point of view, the content was really not that interesting to deliver.

I wasn't learning anything about the people who were attending, and I also wasn't taking advantage of the fact that we had some smart people in the room who we could have been learning from as we went. It was time for a rethink.

I redesigned the workshop from the bottom up with the goal of getting people to really understand the 'why' behind Agglomeration™ and AVC. We were now receiving requests to set up these agglomerations on markets all over the world. Obviously, we couldn't be on the boards of all of them. I was trying to realise the objective of how to train people to a level where we would be comfortable with them representing the Agglomeration™ model on the board of directors. We had spent a long time designing the Agglomeration™ to be as impervious as possible to the risk of bad board members trying to subvert the model to their own selfish ends, but the ideal scenario was always to get the right people on board in the first place.

The reality was that tactics change over time in response to new situations, so it was critical that our key stakeholders, and potentially guardians of this idea moving forward, understood the core philosophies that led to its creation: the 'magnetic north' that would guide the model.

The resulting workshop is a game simulation of what it is like to be a PLC director of a brand-new Agglomeration™ listing. Each participant begins the day at 9am as a director of a new listing. Their objective is to build a $1 bn market cap entity over thirty-six months (the course of the day). They design their perfect board, pick which markets to list on, identify their clients, do pitches encouraging investors and pitches designed for business owners. There are numerous twists and turns along the way including dealing with accidental insider trading, uncooperative companies, exceeding targets and also having to have hard conversations when things go wrong. Where appropriate, I contribute with our own real experiences and why we have chosen to make the choices we have through the benefit of experience.

Interspersed throughout and at the end, we review everything that gets thrown up and then use the remainder of the time to cover individual questions and anything that needs deeper exploration.

The results have been unanimous. Forced to think through situations under time pressure and see things through other people's lenses, the day is filled with 'aha' moments and paradigm shifts that lead to a much deeper understanding of the model. It is also fascinating for everyone involved to see how other people react under pressure. Someone with a traditional finance/investment background reacts very differently to challenges to someone who has been building businesses for several decades.

Agglomerations don't happen in a vacuum, and it is powerful to be able to see the responses of both fellow board members and the market itself to the decisions that individuals make and for us it gives a clear indication of what these individuals would be like to work with, should we choose to, in the future.

There are normally one or two people at the start of each day who think they are too 'grown up' to play a game. But the more you understand the markets, the more you realise it *is* all a game. And more specifically, there are games within the game. The challenge is having the strength and fortitude of mind to keep playing your game while all around you there are people playing different games.

Look at the best investors – for example, Warren Buffett. His greatest strength is his ability to ignore people who are playing a different game and instead stay resolutely focused on his own game. How many

THE 'HOLY GRAIL' OF INVESTING

times have people written him off? During the dot-com years, barely a day passed without some article deriding him for not investing in tech stocks.[20] After the global financial crisis and bull run driven by growth stocks, again there were people questioning his philosophy and his results. But over the longer term he outplays them all. An interesting question now is whether his legacy and philosophy within Berkshire will be strong enough for those returns to continue once he and Charlie Munger finally give up the day job.

One of my favourite quotes from him comes after Amazon CEO Jeff Bezos asked him this question: '[Your strategy] … is so simple. Why doesn't everyone just copy you?' Buffett responded, 'Because nobody wants to get rich slow.'[21]

Know the rules of your game and play to win.

Phoenix time! MBH Corporation PLC

Despite the setback of our first attempt at Agglomeration™, we were in no doubt that the small businesses

---

20 David Schepp, 'Warren Buffett: "I told you so"', BBC News/Business (2001), http://news.bbc.co.uk/2/hi/business/1217716.stm
21 Ahmed Shaami, 'Warren Buffett: Nobody wants to get rich slow', *Being Guru* (2019), www.beingguru.com/2019/05/warren-buffett-nobody-wants-to-get-rich-slow

we knew needed a solution like Agglomeration™ and we felt that if we didn't keep pursuing it, there were very few who had the knowledge and the experience to build this properly in the future. It is a funny thing about 'failure' when trying something new – you almost feel you owe it to others to capitalise on that learning and try again. Otherwise, it is merely a very expensive theoretical lesson.

We knew small businesses needed it, we had also spent enough time with investors to understand that a big enough section of them also understood what we were trying to do and were willing to back it. Our next Agglomeration™ would be called 'MBH Corporation PLC' with the MBH standing for 'Multiple Business Holdings'. The model itself might be creative but with The Marketing Group (TMG) and MBH we certainly weren't going to win any prizes for creativity in naming!

While MBH had lots of subtle changes to our first iteration, the most noticeable to the outside world was that we moved from being a single industry group to a group of diversified industries.

Cycles matter

One of the reasons we choose to go 'sector diversified' in the companies that we acquire is that cycles are important. It doesn't matter how many great, cash-rich companies we bring into the group, if the industry is going through a downturn, we may well look great in comparison to our peers but overall the share price is not going to look that healthy. Macro cycles also matter. Timing is important.

It's worth having a look at another famous diversified group of companies, General Electric (GE). Jack Welch may well have been the greatest CEO of all time (for millennial readers, Jack Welch was the CEO of GE and took an already successful but slightly unwieldy conglomerate and turned it into a stock market darling between 1983 and 2000). He definitely made some hard and controversial decisions that paid handsomely, but since we're talking about timing cycles, let's also note that his tenure coincided with a period of predominantly positive market growth.

In the first eighteen months of his tenure, he did some pretty aggressive things, selling off seventy-one businesses in his famous decision to be first or second in every industry or get out of it. But the stock market barely noticed. Then began one of the biggest bull runs in history with the S&P500 returning some 2,400% over eighteen years.[22] GE almost doubled that in the full twenty years that Jack was in charge, but

---

22 Joe Nocera, 'Was Jack Welch Really That Good?', MSN News (2019), www.msn.com/en-us/news/money/was-jack-welch-really-that-good/ar-AACLCns

would he be remembered so fondly if he had merely outperformed a flat market? Or stayed flat in a down market? Capital allocation is the key responsibility of the CEO, but cycles matter and that is outside the control of any one individual.

An Agglomeration™ cannot pick its timing on a macro level but it can learn from others that have come before. Remember in the first section we looked at Teledyne, a company that acquired 130 businesses in its first decade on the public markets. Unlike Jack Welch, Henry Singleton was still at the head of Teledyne when the market turned against the company in the 1970s. He was forced to change his strategy as the bull market turned bearish. Rather than using his stock to acquire more companies, he decided to utilise his cash to acquire his stock. Over the next decade or so, he bought back almost all of the stock available, exploding his earnings per share from \$8.55 to \$353![23] The average price he paid for his own stock? Eight times earnings. (Remember he had previously been buying other companies at twelve times when he was trading at twenty-five times.)

Had you bought Teledyne Stock and held it for the next fifteen years, you would have outperformed the S&P500 by two and a half times.

---

23 The Investor's Field Guide, 'Shrinkage vs. Growth' (2019), http://investorfieldguide.com/shrinkage-vs-growth

In effect, Teledyne, like an Agglomeration™, is a value investor, acquiring companies that are undervalued compared to the value of their stock. In the event the stock becomes undervalued you just turn the strategy in on itself until the market recovers. The idea was smart, the execution was fantastic but the willingness to pivot to a new strategy when the macroeconomic situation changed is what makes this example stand out.

I'm not smart enough to try and pick the timing of industry or economic cycles and so I don't try. In 2015/16, I remember many people far more learned than me, telling me that listing at the end of the bull run was crazy. Four years later, it seems to still be going. Rather than try and time it, I think having strategies for dealing with both bull and bear seems wise.

So MBH went to market very overtly to become a 'diversified investment holding group'. There were three key thoughts behind this. The first was that the diversification gave protection to all our shareholders in the event that any industry in the group had a downturn. The second was that by not being tied to any one industry, our ability to add companies to the group was increased exponentially. We now had a much wider pool to fish in. And the third was that in the event that our share price ever came under too much pressure again, we would potentially be able to carve out all the companies of one industry into their

IPO. This is just a further protection to all shareholders and has often been shown to create value on both sides of the equation. The holding company shares go up after the carve-out and the new listing is looked upon favourably too.

'Mini Berkshire Hathaway'

Early on in our planning for MBH one of our investors, upon hearing the story of our 'buy and hold' strategy and not interfering with the individual companies, likened us to Berkshire Hathaway. Famously, Warren Buffett has been able to attract great, family-owned businesses to his group because he gave them the autonomy to keep doing what they had always been doing. Our investor joked that MBH should stand for 'Mini Berkshire Hathaway', with an emphasis on the 'mini'. I'm not sure Mr Buffett or Mr Munger would approve, but what started as an off-the-cuff comment has been picked up countless times by the media and I can't really imagine a better brand comparison for us![24]

CASE STUDY: MULTIPLE BUSINESS HOLDINGS (AKA MINI BERKSHIRE HATHAWAY)

Writing a case study about any fast-growth business is always a challenge as in most cases it is completely

---

24 Media links provided in Appendix.

out of date before the first draft is edited, let alone by the time you get round to reading it. But I will provide the background to the business, the philosophy that underpins it and then you can go and check on Bloomberg (https://bloomberg.com/quote/M8H:GR) or our website (www.mbhcorporation.com) to see whether the model has delivered all that we promised!

I will end this case study with my original letter to shareholders when we first did our uplist to the Frankfurt Stock Exchange as it is the best summary of our thinking and what we are trying to achieve, but before I do so, let me just cover the first three businesses and our decision to be a UK PLC listed on a German Stock Exchange.

Was ist das?

After the challenges with our first listing, we knew that, for our next one, we wanted to give ourselves the best possible chance of success, and that meant making some hard decisions. As tempting as it was to go for another unregulated market like the European Nasdaq had been (it is quicker and a lot cheaper), we knew that to build trust we needed to be on a main market. The two obvious ones would be London or New York. However, we were too small for New York (plus we didn't consider the US markets to be very friendly to small caps) and the London Stock Exchange regulations didn't work for our model. Firstly, in London you need to demonstrate a centralised management structure (ours is the ultimate in decentralised models). And even more importantly, in London, as in many main markets, you cannot issue more than 20% of your market cap in newly issued stock in a year without delisting and reissuing a prospectus. Obviously with the Agglomeration™ model, we could find ourselves doing that on a monthly basis. The initial MBH prospectus that we created (which is available at mbhcorporation.com/investors) involved just three companies, had 400 pages and took five months to be approved. The thought of having to do that every month or two would kill the model. Or at the very least, my will to live!

So, the third choice was Frankfurt. It is highly regarded as one of the biggest main markets in the world and is also very liquid (volume of stocks traded each day). But more importantly for us, it had the flexibility of regulation to allow us to pursue the Agglomeration™ model. It would also, automatically, get us on the Xetra – the electronic trading board – allowing us to be traded from anywhere in the world (the downside with unregulated markets is that often, to trade their stocks, you need to open a trading account in the home country, making it sufficiently annoying that most investors won't).

With the market selected, we now looked at a strategy for getting onto it. Our investment bank came up with a route that they thought would save us some time. Basically, you cannot list an empty shell company on Frankfurt, but you can on Dusseldorf. You can then back in the first few companies, issue a prospectus and then use the passport that affords to dual list in Frankfurt. This was a pretty smart solution, although as it turned out the United Kingdom Listing Authority (UKLA) took such a long time approving the prospectus we probably would have been quicker going direct.

Either way, at the end of November 2018, MBH, comprising three great (and very patient) small businesses, was finally listed in Frankfurt. (To learn more about the initial three companies, the original prospectus is still on our website: mbhcorporation.com/investors)

Within a few weeks we did our first listing, acquiring a forty-six-year-old interior fitout company, DuBoulay, which specialised in doing high-end fitouts with a client roster including Fortnum & Mason.

Listing three great companies and then demonstrating our ability to bring in a fourth so quickly was met with … a deafening silence from the German market. Unlike our first listing, where people were clamouring to own our shares and every acquisition would boost the share price, in Germany our first acquisition was met with complete apathy. On most days not a single share was even traded.

While this wasn't ideal, it wasn't totally unexpected either. As a company we had decided very early on that we weren't going to hype the stock – we would much rather deliver and then talk about what we had done. So rather than panic, we decided to spend the next quarter building more awareness among the investor community of what we were doing and what was in our group. It became apparent very quickly that because of the length of time the prospectus had taken, no investors were willing to take a punt on three or four small businesses when the only audited numbers they could look at were from 2017.

Around April 2019, we released our 2018 numbers and it was like a switch had been flicked. With reliable numbers to look at, plus our cumulative marketing and investor relations efforts, we were finally starting to see some traffic in the stock and once again could get busy doing acquisitions.

Over the next few months we announced acquisitions of three more companies. Some were small, others, like Apev (an engineering company out of Singapore), were at the upper end of the size of deals we would expect to do in our first year. Combined, at the end of our first year, the pro forma numbers for what we had in our group had more than tripled to nearly GBP100m in revenue and around GBP9m in ebitda.

Our next big milestone was releasing our 2019 first-half numbers. Although it's not critical to the model, it was nice to be able to demonstrate to the market that the companies in our group were all thriving, and numbers were up across the board. At this point, we were already one of the most heavily traded micro-caps on the Frankfurt market, which was a positive, as less-patient investors were replaced with others who wanted to be a part of our growth in the future. The companies in the group are great and are thriving. The pipeline of companies waiting to join is growing every day. Probably the only thing still on the checklist is to pay our first dividend but it's certainly our intention to pay dividends every year we can.

Only time will tell what the future will bring. There are many elements still outside our control, but we have built about as good a foundation as we can wish for to move forward. It is the job of the companies in the group to keep doing what they are so good at, and for those of us privileged enough to be on the board to keep focused on the fundamentals and sharing the story as we have done through the first year.

Here is my full message to investors when we uplisted to Frankfurt.[25]

Chairman's Letter 2018

To those holding stock or those thinking about it: 2018 is probably the most exciting time in history to be alive for entrepreneurs. There have never been more customers, more resources and more talented people available on the planet than there are today. It is also a time of huge disruption. Technology and demographics are changing the world around us at an incredible pace. For many that change is scary, for entrepreneurs that change offers huge opportunities. While the media focuses on spotty young entrepreneurs creating digital unicorns in their bedrooms, that is not where the majority of value is being created. And yet where the value is being created is a section of the market that is mostly overlooked.

Small to medium enterprises make up 50% of GDP in most developed countries yet remain off limits to investors. These are business owners, men and women, with decades of experience in their industry who have already figured out 'the client/product fit' and their own 'unique selling proposition'. They provide childcare

---

25 Callum Laing, Chairman's Letter 2018, MBH Corporation (2018), www.mbhcorporation.com/chairmans-letter. Some edits have been made to the original message to accommodate it within this publication. Original available at the link above.

to children. Build houses for families and cook meals for hungry people. They don't rely on eyeballs, growth hacking or crypto pump and dump schemes. They sell a good service for money. And weirdly many of them make profits too, year after year! And yet this little-known and profitable section of the market known as SME has previously remained off limits to intelligent investors. Too illiquid and too risky. Many of us have been burnt investing in a friend's new business with a promise of an exit in three to five years. Those that have actually got that result are almost as rare as the unicorns mentioned above.

MBH Corporation PLC now provides a way to reconnect investors with the opportunity in a way that minimises risk and maximises liquidity. Allowing intelligent investors to once again support small businesses but in a way that offers the upside of 'scale-ups' with a more predictable and investor friendly approach. MBH Corporation PLC is probably unlike any other investment you hold, and I therefore believe it is important to clearly articulate our approach, our values and our objectives. The board and the subsidiaries are aligned in their expectations; I believe it is important that all owners of the stock are too. Our structure and our philosophy around growth and increasing shareholder value give us a unique and very flexible tool with which to approach the market. Our decentralised approach, allowing the entrepreneurs that built their businesses to continue to grow them in the way they see fit, allows us unparalleled flexibility to scale and to bring disparate businesses from different sectors and geographies under one holding group to provide maximum protection for all owners.

For the founders of these businesses, merely being part of a PLC levels the playing field with the big corporates they are competing against. This, in and of itself, should lead to organic growth. However, we are not dependent on that as we can develop the group even faster through our steady and consistent acquisition strategy. Our ultimate aim being to end up with many of the best small businesses across multiple sectors and geographies.

Our model

MBH will use the Agglomeration™ model. Since this is so integral to the business of MBH, I will endeavour to explain it. For MBH to achieve its economic objectives, it will identify and acquire good, well-run, profitable and debt-free small businesses. This is probably a good time to describe what we are not. Unlike traditional models, we are neither looking to 'strip and flip' the businesses we acquire, nor are we interested in proving our managerial chops by buying struggling businesses and hoping we can turn them around where others have failed. Finally, we have no desire to merge all the businesses in our group into one cohesive brand with a centralised command and control structure.

The businesses that join us are many years old, with a good track record of profits and typically still run by the founder who often has decades of experience in their industry. Inevitably before finding us, these founders will have talked to other buyers in the marketplace. Big competitors, private equity firms and the like. The reason they are still independent when they come to us is that they value their independence. They like the way they do business, they like their team and the way it works together. Their brand might not mean much outside of their country or even their niche, but it is their brand and their clients trust it. They have no interest in selling to others but will come to MBH because we allow them to scale in their own way. Ensuring that we keep that promise to the founders that join is the key to attracting them and the result of attracting them offers MBH the chance to arbitrage the price a small business can be acquired for and the price a big PLC typically trades at. Therefore, our primary purpose of existence is to provide a platform for those excellent, cash producing businesses to thrive under the ownership of MBH.

Equally we are not actually offering these business owners an 'exit' and therefore do not get drawn into conversations about exit valuations. If founders want to sell their business and leave, there are other options out there. We are most definitely not that solution, but we are a fantastic platform for those that want to scale. This model may not be common, but there are others that have done similar business models with much success and indeed myself and many of the team involved have also worked on this model in the past. An important part to the puzzle is that in almost every case we will be doing our acquisitions using stock to compensate the founders joining us. While the constant creation of shares is dilutive, each acquisition will be EPS accretive and we believe offers greater long-term value creation for shareholders than using cash. As entrepreneurs ourselves, we are all too aware of keeping cash on hand in case things don't go to plan. The entrepreneurs that join us are not looking to exit, indeed if they were, they might find our initial price at which they swap their stock to be poor compensation for the value they have created thus far. Our model provides an 'earn in' approach where the more profit they contribute to the holding company over time, the more shares they earn. While not looking for an exit, the companies that join are ambitious. They are looking to scale, and they know that they can achieve more under the umbrella of a big PLC than on their own. The continuity that we offer them, the ability to get on with the business in hand without worrying about rebranding, or merging with an unknown quantity, allows the founder and their team to keep their focus on the business they are building. This continuity offers us a competitive advantage and is one that is fundamental to our business.

Our model is ultimately then very simple. Allow good, well-run businesses to swap their private shares for public shares but continue to run their business as before. As co-owners of MBH, they too benefit when we bring in other companies and enjoy the value creation afforded to us in the P/E arbitrage. As companies come in, they will sit within verticals under the main holding company. There are no limits to the number of verticals we can create and the benefit that brings to existing companies. Because of our approach, most of the shareholders in MBH are the founders themselves and they have full visibility of their own contribution and the contribution of the other founders across the group. Those 'new' investors who we are now talking to as part of going public will be owners, alongside the founders, in the holding company and while we might occasionally share case studies of the companies within, the focus will be the consolidated numbers of the group. This gives each founder the confidence to continue to make the right decisions about reinvesting profits where they believe the long-term benefit exists to do so.

This model is not for every business out there. 'Debt free, profitable and well run' already rules out most. Some would choose to go the IPO route alone, still others have trouble believing in a collaborative approach to anything and a third group understands the appeal but don't yet feel they are ready to join. This is fine, just through our own network we know of several hundred companies that do fit our criteria and have expressed an interest in joining. In our experience, companies have a habit of showing up, when the founder is ready. This model allows us enormous flexibility to work with great companies regardless of sector or territory as long as it enhances shareholder value.

The value of Agglomeration™

Can we have universal values when each company that joins has its own unique culture and values? Especially when we emphasise their own independence? We believe so and you'll see that not only do our values make perfect sense in the context of what we are trying to achieve, they tend to attract companies, and hopefully investors, who share those values.

Trust. As entrepreneurs ourselves we trust other entrepreneurs to do what is right to continue to build value for their clients and their teams. In our belief you get better results, especially with entrepreneurs, when you give control rather than try and take control. If someone has proven they can build a debt-free, profitable business and believes ours is the best platform to allow them to scale that business, we owe it to them to trust that they will continue to make the right decisions. While a centralised command and control strategy looks great on paper, we don't believe it offers the best solution in today's dynamic environment. However, trust does not mean irresponsibility. The companies joining will be fully audited with full due diligence by two outside entities. Unlike others, we are not taking punts on early-stage businesses, the businesses we work with are proven.

Velocity. When you trust the team you work with, it allows you to move fast and make quick decisions. The only competitive advantage a small business really has over a big corporation is its ability to make quick decisions and act on them. The fear is always that it may lead to mistakes and of course it will. But then there are plenty of committees that slow things down and still make the wrong decision. When mistakes are made, as they always will be, the temptation is to start adding rules. Before long you are a bureaucracy where common sense is a diminishing value. The only effective counter to this, and the only way to capitalise on moving fast, is to trust your team. See 'Trust', above.

Collaboration. We believe that the business world is evolving from an era of competition to an era of collaboration. The Agglomeration™ is the ultimate form of collaborative IPO for small businesses, but it is also indicative of a mindset that focuses on solutions not problems, that emphasises empathy over confrontation. We use the analogy of pulling your chair round to the other side of the table in order to see what the other person sees. How do we get to a solution together?

Of course, when you trust each other and are willing to collaborate, the whole business can move at a much higher velocity.

MBH offers to business owners a solution that few others can offer. A platform to scale and the autonomy to do so in the way they feel is best. But our values are an integral part of that. Firstly, this model doesn't appeal to all and so in many ways it is self-selecting, but we are genuinely drawn to honourable entrepreneurs, the kind you would be happy to take home and introduce to your mum. Through our own reputations and those that we bring in, it gets easier to attract good people.

It may strike others as old-fashioned, but these are the people we want to work with, the ones we want owning our stock and ultimately guiding this group in the future. If those values don't resonate with you, there are probably better stocks out there for you to own ...

How we measure success

Scale, earnings per share, organic growth and synergies

MBH is designed to scale. The systems have been built specifically to allow the persistent and high velocity approach to scale through acquisition. You will notice that much of the focus in the first two to three years will indeed be about the scale. New countries, new verticals, and – if we do our job right – a steadily, if not rapidly, increasing ebitda and net cash position (usual disclaimers apply).

Earnings per share is the metric we choose to focus on. As mentioned above, we would never do an acquisition into the main group that wasn't EPS accretive in nature. Obviously, we will continue to provide as much data as possible to our sophisticated investors who will choose to do their own analysis, but in our opinion, EPS is the most prudent measure.

Beyond scale and EPS we must talk about organic growth. MBH exists to support small businesses that want to scale. If we fail to do that then we are purely an arbitrage between private and public markets. It would still serve a valuable purpose, providing liquidity for founders in small business and allowing investors to reconnect with this valuable part of the economy. However, if companies are not thriving in this environment we create, then we are not delivering on our full potential.

From an investment standpoint it should be acknowledged upfront that scaling takes resources and it is rare for a small business to be able to scale significantly while increasing their free cash. While we would hope to see signs of scaling pretty quickly upon joining our group, it is unlikely that this will translate into significantly more profits up to the holding company in the short term. However, due to the nature of the 'earn in' structure, it is unlikely to signal much of a reduction either.

Small business struggles for many reasons. Credibility, attracting talented staff, ability to retain or attract those staff, inability to go for large projects, and so on. All of these are issues that should be mitigated when companies join us.

Synergies are rarely the panacea that people want them to be, yet as the number of companies in MBH moves into double and triple figures over the years, the opportunities for companies to work together will likely prove irresistible to the founders who join. Our job at board level is not to foist synergies and partnerships upon the subsidiaries, but it is most definitely to facilitate the transference of ideas and opportunities between those companies in the group. Indeed, many companies will join specifically because they wish to join such an entrepreneurial environment.

Our fantastically talented and able Allan Presland serves as CEO for (rather than of) those companies to act as chief collaborator and help facilitate those opportunities to work together, yet ultimately the final decision will come down to the individual founders. Is my team ready for this? Does it really add value to my clients? If they feel it is not right, they will be perfectly entitled to continue to run their business in the way they always have.

(Of course, we will occasionally be sure to cherry-pick the best of these synergistic success stories and share them with you as though it was our plan all along!)

Organic growth, then, is unlikely to show up in the first quarter, it might not even show up in the first year, but if companies are not growing organically by their second year, we will need to investigate how we can improve this area. MBH should serve as an incubator to growth.

The companies in MBH

In the media there is much talk that entrepreneurs should follow their 'passion'. However, when pressed, the premise doesn't hold much water. The market has no interest in what you are passionate about, it only cares about how you can create value. It certainly helps with your persistence if you are passionate about it, but it's not the defining metric people seem to think.

Perhaps a more useful metric for those starting out is who are the type of people you are passionate about creating value for? Figure that out and your entrepreneurial journey will be much more enjoyable, if not much easier.

In this we most definitely eat our own dogfood. Entrepreneurs/small business owners are our people. We understand them, we know the sleepless nights they have and why they do it. We know how personally they take a customer complaint while ignoring the hundreds of positive things people say. And we know and appreciate the way they make the hard decisions with their team to build a business all can be proud of.

These are our people; they are the ones we want running our companies and they are the ones we want standing shoulder to shoulder with us as owners of MBH. MBH is a company built by entrepreneurs for entrepreneurs. Those who join us care more deeply about the future of their business than purely the 'price' offered. So do we.

You

By definition, when we take MBH public we invite in 'the public', yet owning MBH stock entitles you to join a particular type of shareholder. The majority of MBH shareholders are the founders. As above, they are the people we not only just want running our companies, they are the type of people we want owning our stock. They are the people we want on the board and shepherding this venture forward long after myself and the initial team have hung up our gloves.

Entrepreneurs spend their lives creating value for others and paying themselves last. While we want them to enjoy the fruits of their labour, these are people who are in this game for the long haul. They believe in their business and they believe in the long-term success of MBH. On the board, we will spend all day, every day, courting investors who share that view. The investors we look for are those who understand our model and the value creation the model can create.

By going public we open ourselves to speculators, but those who make short-term bets are, in our opinion, missing the bigger picture and opportunity.

It takes time for investors to understand what we are doing; we want to retain them and help them benefit over the long term. Entrepreneurs are terrible at overestimating how much they can achieve in a year and underestimating what they can achieve in ten. We fear many investors share a similar curse.

We are seeking owners who understand small business, understand the principles we share and want to come along on this journey. We are not looking for those who want to be diving in and out of the stock hourly on the basis of the latest ill-informed forum gossip. If placing your faith in proven entrepreneurs makes you feel uncomfortable, this stock is most definitely not for you.

A piece of ownership and volatility

The nature of the MBH stock, with the majority being locked up by the founders/owners, means that the remaining public stock can be quite volatile despite our best efforts. As entrepreneurs ourselves, we are dynamic and opportunistic. While the price is high, we will certainly increase our acquisition activities, while it is low, we are likely to buy back stock for future use.

However, like any good entrepreneurs we will focus on what we can control, not what is outside of our control. EPS is what you will find the board and the subsidiaries coming back to time and time again. The share price is a necessary distraction, and not one we will be likely to comment on in the future so I shall keep my thoughts on this succinct.

In an ideal world and a perfect market, the share price would edge up quarter on quarter in lockstep with the EPS we report and the additional profit we bring in with our acquisitions. That is, of course, not the world we live in and both high and low share prices can cause us some challenges. Too high and we risk our owners taking profits off the table. While I can't blame them for doing so, the problem is they are much more likely to sell those shares to speculators. It takes a long time to find co-owners who we like, respect and who share our long-term values. Replacing them, however slowly, with speculators changes the dynamic for all remaining shareholders.

Too low a share price is a more common concern from PLCs and of course it makes it harder for us to do our job, but it is by no means critical to the model and may indeed prompt the board to do a share buy-back to keep things more steady and allow us to continue our growth path. Regardless of our wants or needs, the share price will fluctuate based on buyers and sellers in the marketplace. For obvious reasons, beyond this letter, we will not be drawn to comment further and will focus instead on executing our plan. It is no secret that the stock price and the intrinsic value of the group will often diverge.

We certainly believe that, over time, this will 'come out in the wash' and the two will converge again. If we can remain focused on creating value, the share price should reflect that in the long term. Despite the potential volatility of limited public stock and the inherent volatility of the small business space, we feel comfortable we can be rather predictable in our growth through acquisition. But even with that, we are no 'traditional' PLC and want investors who are able to weather the bumps in the road in order to enjoy the journey. The business has solid foundations: debt-free, profitable companies across multiple sectors and territories.

We will continue to add to that, creating a powerful business built for the long-term growth and success of the subsidiaries within.

The future and human nature

When discussing this model, we are often asked what is the target number of businesses. What does it look like in the future?

Certainly, the board is committed to fast and manageable growth over the next two to three years. We believe that is the best, and ultimately safest, approach for all involved. When the number of subsidiaries in the group hits certain internal targets on scale we may, in consultation with the founders, look at changing the nature of the businesses we bring in or exploring other options, perhaps to spin off one of the verticals in its own IPO. Because we are only working with debt-free and profitable companies and they maintain their independence, there is no point when we could not put acquisitions on hold and 'coast' for a while if that is deemed to be in the best interests of all.

However, what we must be cognisant of is the human nature to slow things down, not as strategy, but as reaction. When working with small businesses there will be challenges. Despite our best efforts, a company that joins the group may struggle, that struggle could take many forms, losing clients, or money, a media snafu. It is tempting when faced with such struggles to put a hold on the current strategy and deal with the issue at hand. Yet the entrepreneurs we work with are successful precisely because of their ability to not get drawn into every problem that arises but instead focus on value creation and delivering the strategy.

On the board, it is our responsibility to not give in to the 'noise' but to keep pressing forward with this unique opportunity to support small business and deliver incredible returns to our co-owners. It is also our responsibility to fight against the market that is more familiar and comfortable with a model where companies are merged, systems are centralised and a mass rebranding sounds like a good idea. We will resist that, despite the pressure, because we believe that we can attract much better businesses into the group by offering them full autonomy to keep delivering value in the way they currently do.

The 1%

Finally, I want to leave you with an idea that probably will tell you more about our values and ethos than the rest of this letter or prospectus put together. Each one of our founders and all our pre-IPO partners/investors are invited to contribute 1% of their stock to go towards worthy causes. Each vertical picks causes that are particular to them. In the childcare vertical it is building schools in developing countries; in property it's building homes. This idea came from the founders themselves and while it's completely voluntary it's always one of the ideas that often gets the most excitement from the companies that join.

The growth and success of MBH thus takes on a much bigger role. Yes, we believe that as the companies in the group grow, they will serve more clients, create more jobs and thus support their communities. But we are also big believers that it is entrepreneurs who are the ultimate change-makers in society. They are the ones who are shaking up philanthropy, who are changing the nature of charity and solving the biggest problems that face the world today.

MBH wants to play its own small part in that and we invite you along too.

Callum Laing

Alpha: Conclusion

I have had the honour of being the face of MBH through its first year of a PLC and it has been an absolute pleasure to do so. I say 'face' and not 'leader' as it is the subsidiary owners, the principals, who are the 'leaders' who actually drive the business. However, I am lucky enough to represent them and to have met countless new businesses that want to join us. I have had the opportunity to share our story with investors all over the world, an enormous percentage of whom have embraced the vision and come on board. Perhaps we have got better at articulating our story (I still think we have a way to go), or perhaps we have got better at targeting the right types of investors (this is definitely true), and the many who have believed in us are now our co-owners in a company that, even with the brakes on in the early days, has tripled in size in its first year and become one of the most heavily traded micro-caps on the German markets.

My job is not to be the face of MBH forever. Right now, it is to get the right people on board the train so that it can continue to gather pace and attract ever more companies and value to the group. Ultimately, I can probably do more to support the business owners and investors by being off the board and focusing on the bigger strategy, but we're not there yet.

We really haven't even got started yet. We still have many more businesses to attract and the opportunities that happen when you have 30, 300 or 3,000 are incredibly exciting to all of us involved.

What about AVC? The focus in our first year was definitely on getting MBH up, running and cracking along at a decent pace, and yet alongside that we did still manage to raise a couple of million in AVC and it did its first investment into DuBoulay just before it was brought into MBH.

As mentioned previously, this book is really the first time we have gone to market with the opportunity of AVC. We believe it will be a complete game-changer for small business when these two entities of

Agglomeration™ and AVC are forging along at full pace, in parallel with each other.

Then investors will truly be able to access the holy trinity of **impact, liquidity** and **alpha**: to become co-owners of agglomerations that are both fast growth and high yielding and to finally reconnect the capital markets with those that create the jobs and contribute so much to the economy.

THE THREE-CIRCLE MODEL

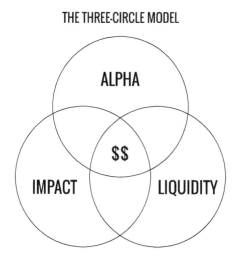

Conclusion

I remember as a young entrepreneur struggling to keep my start-up afloat and yet at the same time I was a member of Toastmasters International – an organisation that creates massive value in the world, that is basically staffed by volunteers, has hundreds of chapters around the world and has survived nearly 100 years. This fascinated me.

It's interesting because the question in business that most people focus on is how does a business grow? How does it thrive? But we should flip that question and instead ask how is it we don't die? How do we survive?

Survival of a business is surely the ultimate goal, so why do some organisations survive beyond their leadership and others fade away once the dynamic leader is no more? In my first book, *Progressive Partnerships*,[26] I talk about the need for even a local club or networking event to have a sustainable revenue model and systems in order to attract the next generation of leadership. I was born in New Zealand, but grew up in Cambridge, England, and was surrounded by universities that had been in existence for hundreds and hundreds of years. Was there anything we could learn from those in order to build an organisation that could last more than a decade?

The reality is that it's a cruel world out there for entrepreneurs, and therefore for investors who place their faith in them. The Bureau of Labor Statistics in the USA keeps a sobering tally of how often businesses fail, and here are the numbers from 1995–2015:

Years in business	Failure rate
1 year	21.2%
2 years	32.1%
5 years	51.2%
10 years	66.6%
20 years	79.6%

(Source: Jeff Desjardins)[27]

26 Callum Laing, *Progressive Partnerships* (Rethink Press Limited, 2016)
27 Jeff Desjardins, 'Here's why small businesses fail', *Business Insider* (2017), www.businessinsider.com/why-small-businesses-fail-infographic-2017-8?r=US&IR=T

One study by a US Bank shows that 82% of small businesses fail because of cashflow mismanagement. This is a fair point, since without cashflow there is no business. But isn't cashflow a symptom of deeper problems?

Martin Reeves, and colleagues, of the BCG Henderson Institute believe that companies should take lessons on adaptability from nature and outline six key areas to think about:[28]

- **Redundancy.** Stuff happens. Being able to reduce the number of single points of failure in your business gives you the best possible chance of lasting longer.

- **Heterogeneity.** Diversity isn't just a politically correct catchphrase; it is absolutely critical to adapting to the fast-changing world we live in. We need diversity of ideas and that will only come from diversity of backgrounds.

- **Modularity.** Creating independence between operating entities in the organisation can help to protect rot from spreading. One bad apple should not be able to ruin the barrel.

- **Adaptability.** In nature it is often said that it is not the best that survives, it is the most adaptable, or

---

28 Martin Reeves, Simon Levin and Daichi Ueda, 'The Biology of Corporate Survival', *Harvard Business Review* (2016), https://hbr. org/2016/01/ the-biology-of-corporate-survival

put another way it is those that can adapt to their environment that *become* the best. Can you create an environment that attracts ideas and innovation (good and bad) and allows the good to thrive?

- **Prudence.** You can't get all the decisions right, but can you minimise those decisions that will risk the company?

- **Embeddedness.** Businesses don't exist in vacuum. Are you supporting and contributing to the community you are in? The more you become a component of other people's success the more people you will have rooting for your success.

It is difficult not to look at that list and overlay it with what we are trying to build with Agglomeration™.

Another interesting thought-leader in this space is Geoffrey West, a 'theoretical physicist-turned-biologist-turned-urbanisation expert'. His team analysed about 30,000 publicly traded companies in the USA over the last sixty years and found that the average lifespan of a company already on the stock exchange is about ten years. Not many last 100, 200 or 300 years and only a very few last 400 years.

What I find interesting about this is that the companies may not have lasted 400 years, but the market itself has. The market doesn't decide which businesses should survive and thrive and which shouldn't, it merely provides a platform. Some do, some don't, but the market is successful as long as it continues to attract new businesses into its ecosystem and provide a service to them.

Why do cities live forever, and companies don't? West argues it has to do with the ability to generate ideas; that we as humans are attracted to the ability to interact with more people and that interaction and diversity creates ideas. As West says, 'If you bring more people together you have more interactions and therefore create more ideas and more wealth. You encourage entrepreneurship and you have this positive feedback loop that is manifested in the scaling laws ... placing emphasis on controlling costs and creating economies of scale.'[29]

Could we not say exactly the same about Agglomeration™? By its very nature an Agglomeration™ will have more brains, from more backgrounds, with more perspectives, yet all working together, or separately, towards a common goal. Increasing the value of the commonly held stock. By creating a platform that allows already successful people to create more success we should end up with the 'positive feedback loop' that West talks about.

29   Christy MacLeod, 'Geoffrey West on the Life and Death of Companies', *Percolate* (2015), https://blog.percolate.com/2015/09/transition-2015-geoffrey-west-on-the-life-and-death-of-companies

We talked earlier about the Agglomeration™ game, so to finish I shall pose the question I set for attendees at the end of each workshop: 'Why do cities seem to last for millennia but companies rarely last more than a decade or two?'

It is a question that I have wrestled with for many years. Or more specifically, I have wrestled with the question of how do you create a multi-generational business? What is it that those that last decades or even centuries do differently from those that start, grow, flame brightly and then fade away? (Or don't even flame brightly before fading away as some of my early ventures did!)

Seth Godin points out that it is the infrastructure that is key.[30] The roads and communal spaces that connect people in a city rarely change but the buildings are frequently replaced over the years. 'When creating an organization, a technology or any kind of culture, the roads are worth far more than the buildings.'

What if we were not to think of Agglomeration™ as a company, but as an ecosystem designed to attract and support the best companies and evolve and mutate over time in response to the environment it finds itself in? Some companies will thrive, others will wither and die over time, but if you have the right 'roads' (or

---

30 Seth Godin, 'Roads or buildings?', *Seth's Blog* (3 June 2019), https://
    seths.blog/2019/06/roads-or-buildings

infrastructure) in place and build the right urban centre, the ecosystem should survive, and you will continue to attract innovation. You don't need to rely on having the smarts in the group to respond to challenges, you can merely bring in those who are already proving they can thrive and give them the support to do more.

What next? A peek into the future

It is of course impossible to know if we will move the needle at all on the challenges that small businesses and investors face. And it is more than unlikely that you or I will still be around in a century or two to see whether this model is as sustainable as we hope.

What we do know is that for the handful of companies that we have worked with so far, we have done some good and created some value. Investors get a chance to own a highly liquid portfolio of small companies with the best possible chance of survival and growth. But will the model be robust enough to survive when we hand it over to the second generation? Of course, we think we have answers to the risks we know, but the biggest risk is the one that has never crossed our minds.

Our best hope for surviving is having well-informed shareholders across the spectrum who are willing to push back on boards that might otherwise lose sight of the long term and are willing to sacrifice it for the short term.

I hope you will join me as one such informed person.

Appendix

Media links to support 'Mini Berkshire Hathaway':

www.yahoo.com/news/warren-buffet-small-business-133000406.html

www.finanztrends.info/mbh-corp-plc-interview-mit-ceo-callum-laing-auf-der-muenchener-kapitalmarkt-konferenz-mkk-2019

www.goingpublic.de/going-public-und-being-public/auch-mittelstaendische-unternehmen-benoetigen-einen-zugang-zum-kapitalmarkt

www.4investors.de/nachrichten/boerse.php?sektion=stock&ID=134948

References

Arnold, Christopher, 'The Foundation for
Economies Worldwide Is Small Business',
IFAC (2019), www.ifac.org / knowledge-
gateway / practice-management / discussion /
foundation-economies-worldwide-small-business

Buffett, Warren, *The Snowball* (Bloomsbury, 2009)

Carlson, Ben, 'How to Win Any Argument
About the Stock Market', *Fortune* (2019),
https: / / fortune.com / 2019 / 06 / 11 /
stock-market-how-to-win-arguments

Channel News Asia, 'Strength in Unity –
Collaborative IPO's, Agglomeration', YouTube
(2016), www.youtube.com / watch?v=e1XgRwHxtwc

Chen, James, 'Alpha', *Investopedia* (2019), www. investopedia.com/terms/a/alpha.asp

Cohan, William D, 'The Michael Milken Project: How did a 70-year-old ex-con barred for life from Wall Street become one of its most respected men?', *Institutional Investor* (2017), www. institutionalinvestor.com/article/b1f6wj9ghqxv8h/ The-Michael-Milken-Project

Desjardins, Jeff, 'Here's why small businesses fail', *Business Insider* (2017), www.businessinsider. com/why-small-businesses-fail-infographic-2017-8?r=US&IR=T

Fitzgerald, Maggie, 'The CEOs of nearly 200 companies just said shareholder value is no longer their main objective', CNBC (2019), www.cnbc.com/ amp/2019/08/19/the-ceos-of-nearly-two-hundred-companies-say-shareholder-value-is-no-longer-their-main-objective.html

Gardner, David and Tom, *The Motley Fool's Rule Breakers, Rule Makers: The Foolish Guide to Picking Stock* (Touchstone, 2010)

Godin, Seth, 'Roads or buildings?', *Seth's Blog* (3 June 2019), https://seths.blog/2019/06/ roads-or-buildings

Harbour, Jeremy and Laing, Callum, *Agglomerate –
Idea to IPO in 12 Months* (Rethink Press Limited, 2016)

Laing, Callum, Chairman's Letter 2018, MBH
Corporation (2018), www.mbhcorporation.com/
chairmans-letter

Laing, Callum, 'Elon Musk', *The Asian Entrepreneur*
(2018), www.asianentrepreneur.org/elon-musk

Laing, Callum, 'Lessons learnt from losing $250m ...',
The Asian Entrepreneur (2017), www.
asianentrepreneur.org/lessons-learnt-losing-250m

Laing, Callum, *Progressive Partnerships* (Rethink Press
Limited, 2016)

Lewis, Michael, *Flashboys* (Penguin, 2015)

MacLeod, Christy, 'Geoffrey West on the Life and
Death of Companies', *Percolate* (2015), https://blog.
percolate.com/2015/09/transition-2015-geoffrey-
west-on-the-life-and-death-of-companies

Macrotrends, www.macrotrends.net/stocks/charts/
AAPL/apple/stock-price-history

Mulcahy, Diane, 'The New Reality of the 14-Year
Venture Capital Fund', *Institutional Investor*
(2015), www.institutionalinvestor.com/article/

b14z9vv7hjbt6y / the-new-reality-of-the-14-year-venture-capital-fund

Nocera, Joe, 'Was Jack Welch Really That Good?', MSN News (2019), www.msn.com / en-us / news / money / was-jack-welch-really-that-good / ar-AACLCns

Reeves, Martin, Levin, Simon, and Ueda, Daichi, 'The Biology of Corporate Survival', *Harvard Business Review* (2016), https:/ / hbr.org / 2016 / 01 / the-biology-of-corporate-survival

Ritter, Jay R, 'Initial Public Offerings: Updated Statistics on Long-run Performance' (2019), https:/ / site.warrington.ufl.edu / ritter / files / 2019 / 04 / IPOs2018_Longrun-Returns.pdf

Schepp, David, 'Warren Buffett: "I told you so"', BBC News / Business (2001), http:/ / news.bbc.co.uk / 2 / hi / business / 1217716.stm

Shiller, Robert J, *Irrational Exuberance: Revised and Expanded Third Edition* (Princeton University Press, 2016)

Shaami, Ahmed, 'Warren Buffett: Nobody wants to get rich slow', *being Guru* (2019), www.beingguru.com / 2019 / 05 / warren-buffett-nobody-wants-to-get-rich-slow

Stewart, James B, *Den of Thieves* (Simon & Schuster Ltd, 1992)

The Investor's Field Guide, 'Shrinkage vs. Growth' (2019), http://investorfieldguide.com/shrinkage-vs-growth

Yitzhak, Yaron, 'This is how rich you'd be if you bought Apple stock instead of its products', *the next web* (2019), https://thenextweb.com/plugged/2019/06/18/this-is-how-rich-youd-be-if-you-bought-apple-stock-instead-of-its-products

Acknowledgements

More than any previous book of mine, this was written on planes between destinations as I have bounced around the globe sharing our story and meeting with fantastic investors and business owners. So, while it feels like I should acknowledge the various crews of Singapore Airlines who have supplied me with endless coffee and snacks to get this complete, it is, of course, my family that deserve the biggest acknowledgement.

My wife won't read this, but she deserves the biggest thanks. I can't imagine doing what I do without her support. Mia, I know you think my books are boring and full of long words. You're probably right. The stories you have written and published by the age of nine are way more entertaining and make me very proud. Ella, whether it's LEGO® houses or digital houses, I can't wait to see what you build next.

None of this would have happened without the core team at Unity Group: Hadi, Muriel, Dinnah, Chee Hao, Luc and Charlotte, you constantly inspire me. Extra-special thanks to Victor whose capacity for work handled without grumble seemingly knows no bounds; Gina who despite having at least three full-time jobs manages to manage me excellently; and, of course, Jeremy who somehow can always find the opportunity and the humour in every challenge. Many thanks.

MBH wouldn't have happened without the patience, dedication and faith of Dave Howes, Vikki Sylvester and Allan Presland. And the board support of Dave Hallam and Toby Street. Thanks to you and all the business owners who have joined since.

AVC could still be on the drawing board without Stephen Fisher and Tony Morgan. Looking forward to great things!

Finally, to all the investors who have already come on board and backed our idea with your hard-earned money, thank you for your support. I can't guarantee the outcome, but I can absolutely guarantee our commitment to working for you.

The Author

Callum Laing has spent more than twenty years as an entrepreneur, ten as an investor and five working on bringing the two subjects together in the public markets through the Agglomeration™ methodology.

Born in New Zealand, raised in Cambridge, England and living in Asia since 2002, Callum is the author of two other books, *Progressive Partnerships: The Future of Business* and *Agglomerate – Idea to IPO in 12 Months*.

An insatiable curiosity for everything business- and investing-related has led to a side project where he has published over one thousand interviews with entrepreneurs, business leaders and investors from Asia and beyond through the platform AsianEntrepreneur.org.

He is founder and CEO of MBH Corporation PLC (www.mbhcorporation.com) and also has roles as an adviser with Kinguin (eGaming), high commissioner with WBAF and ambassador with DealGateway.com.

Together with his business partner Jeremy Harbour he regularly speaks all over the world at harbourclubevents.com and other such events.

He lives in Singapore with his wife and two daughters.

Follow him on LinkedIn.com/in/CallumLaing and Twitter.com/LaingCallum or to sign up for a newsletter at CallumLaing.com.

The Agglomeration™ workshop

Having read this book, if you would like to know more about being the director of a public company running an Agglomeration™ and join other like-minded business owners and investors for a fully immersive training programme, register for the Agglomeration™ workshop.

www.unity-group.com/agglomeration-workshop

If you have got some value from reading this book and are able to join others in leaving a review on amazon.com, you can make a direct impact on the lives of children in developing nations. Through working with b1g1.com, I make a monthly contribution of school books for every review any of my books receive – good, bad or ugly!

Thank you
Callum Laing

Lightning Source UK Ltd.
Milton Keynes UK
UKHW011419030520
362587UK00010B/769